KASHMIR
A Young Thinkers' Perspective

KASHMIR
A Young Thinkers' Perspective

Edited by

Aaditya Tiwari

PENTAGON PRESS LLP

KASHMIR: A Young Thinkers' Perspective
Edited by Aaditya Tiwari

First Published in 2022

Copyright © India Foundation, New Delhi

ISBN 978-93-90095-63-6

All rights reserved. No part of this publication may be reproduced, stored in a retrieval system, or transmitted, in any form or by any means, electronic, mechanical, photocopying, recording, or otherwise, without first obtaining written permission of the copyright owner.

Disclaimer: The views and opinions expressed in the book are the individual assertion of the respective Authors in their personal capacity and do not have any official endorsement. Moreover the Publisher does not take any responsibility for the same in any manner whatsoever. Attributability of the contents lies purely with Author.

Published by
PENTAGON PRESS LLP
206, Peacock Lane, Shahpur Jat
New Delhi-110049
Phones: 011-64706243, 26491568
Telefax: 011-26490600
email: rajan@pentagonpress.in
website: www.pentagonpress.in

Printed at Aegean Offset Printers, Greater Noida, U.P.

Contents

	Preface: Kashmir: Past, Present, and Future *Maj Gen Dhruv C Katoch, SM, VSM*	vii
	Contributors	xxiii
1.	Ten Years of the Young Thinkers Meet (YTM) *Aaditya Tiwari*	1
2.	Evolving Security Dynamics of J&K *Soumya Chaturvedi*	7
3.	Reflections on Kashmir *Ajit Datta*	15
4.	My Tryst with Kashmir post the Abrogation of Article 370 *Dhairya Roy*	21
5.	Knowing Kashmir and Kashmiris *Hamsa Devineni*	26
6.	Kashmir: A battle against known unknowns *Abhishek Malhotra*	30
7.	Developments in Jammu & Kashmir: A Kaleidoscopic Viewpoint *Nidhi Vyas*	35

8.	"Know Kashmir" Beyond Article 370 *Sammridh Varma*	38
9.	Kashmir, Development and Dignity: An Analysis *Dr. Abhishek Pratap Singh*	42
10.	Scrapping Article 370 has Evolved a Vision and Environment for Better Healthcare in Naya Kashmir *Dr. Aakansha Bhawsar*	48
11.	I am Gupkar Road! *Ujjwal Virendra Deepak and Ashutosh Dubey*	53
12.	Charting an Investment Roadmap for Jammu and Kashmir *Mishika Nayyar*	57
13.	The Grey Saffron: Journey of Kashmir from Political Separatism to Religious Separatism *Swayam Prakash Baral*	67
14.	Experience of Kashmir Hitherto seen only on Maps *Chiranjeevi Bhat*	71
15.	From Ideological Saffron to Kashmiri Saffron *Aparajita Tripathi*	78
16.	Report Tenth Young Thinkers Meet	98
	Index	122

Preface
Kashmir: Past, Present, and Future[1]

Maj Gen Dhruv C Katoch, SM, VSM

It is important to understand the historical undercurrents which drive a society to look for its roots. It is equally important to delve into history to see that no set of actors try to misappropriate the legacy of a people by false analogies. Towards the latter end, a deliberate attempt is being made by some motivated groups with a fixed agenda, to portray Kashmir as an entity, which has historically been separate from India. Such falsehoods, fortunately, cannot stand historical scrutiny. Kashmir is not just an integral part of India, but is its very soul.

Since time immemorial, the majestic Himalayas have been part of the Indian social, cultural and spiritual milieu. Ancient Indian religious texts such as the Vishnu, Shiv and Matsya Puranas, as well as the great spiritual epic, the Mahabharata, make constant mention of the Himalayas, and in their description of Bharat, define it as the land lying between the Himalayas to the North and the Ocean in the South.[2] The Markandeya Puraan describes the land mass of

Bharat as "the land that is girdled by the sea on three sides and on the North by the Himalayas, which stretch like the string of a bow".[3] In the Vishnu Puraan, the people who live in this geographical area, north of the oceans and South of the Himalayas, are described as Bharatiyas, in a beautiful couplet as under:

> *'Uttaram yat samudrasya, Himadreshchaiv dakshinam, varsham tad bharatam nama, Bharatee yatra santatihi'.*

That the people of this land were bound together by a common spiritual tradition was also noted by India's first prime minister, Shri JL Nehru, in his 'Discovery of India,' who wrote of *'the uniqueness about this continuity of a cultural tradition through five thousand years of history, of invasion and upheaval, a tradition which was widespread among the masses and powerfully influenced them'*.[4] Since millennia, sages in India have walked the length and breadth of this land, from North to South and from East to West. Tamil poets from early times have made mention of the Northern extent of Bharat as the land which is the abode of Siva and the 'tapovan' (Sanskrit: austerity and spiritual practices) of saints and seers.[5] The centrality of the Himalayas, in India's social and spiritual construct is thus not a modern phenomenon, but is deeply rooted in the psyche of the people—a construct synthesised and refined over thousands of years, and passed on from one generation to the next. That is why, ancients texts make constant reference to the *'Kashmir Mandala'* in terms of its spatial and temporal locus as part of India's sacred geography. Kashmir is hence described, not just as India's northernmost outpost, but as the very fountainhead of Indian culture—indeed, as the very soul of India.

It is important to understand this historicity, to better appreciate the vicious manner in which attempts are now being made by certain vested interests to portray Kashmir as a land which was never a part of the Indian imagination. The Great Mauryan empire, in its vast spread, encompassed both Kashmir to the North and present day Afghanistan to its West. During the reign of Ashoka, a complete system of administration was established in Kashmir. For Bharat, the Himalayas did not just provide a formidable natural line of defence; these sacred mountains were and are the core of India's spiritual thought. Kashmir, nestled in the lap of the Himalayas, thus became a focal point for the spread of Indian culture to Central, East and Southeast Asia. Straddling the communication network between Central Asia, Afghanistan and China, the region gained strategic significance and in the early years of the 19th century, became the foci of the rivalry played out between Czarist Russia and Imperial Britain, which came to be known as the Great Game.

The Beginning of the Sultanate

In the first quarter of the 14th century, the Mongols invaded the land. This invasion was the beginning of the tumultuous events that were to overtake the Kashmir Valley over the next 400 years. After ravaging the land for eight months, the Mongols left before the onset of winter. The ruler at that time was King Suhadeva, who attempted appeasement of the invaders by way of expensive gifts, but these were spurned by the Mongol army which continued its spree of killings, loot and plunder. The King died soon after and his place was taken by his Prime Minister, Ram Chander, who in turn appointed Rinchan, a Buddhist prince from Ladakh, as an administrator. Rinchan soon gained the confidence of the

Raja and then treacherously killed him, and anointed himself as the ruler in 1320 CE.[6] At this point of time, the history of Kashmir took a dramatic turn. Rinchan had married Ram Chander's daughter and desired to convert to Hinduism, but the head priest of the Brahmin Pandit's Devaswami denied the newly anointed Raja his request. As a result, Rinchan converted to Islam and adopted the title of Sultan Sadruddin Shah. 10,000 of his subjects converted along with him.[7]

Rinchan died three years later, in 1323 CE. He founded a quarter in Srinagar called Rinchanpura on his name and built a mosque, Bud Masjid, on the site of a Buddhist temple. With his death, Kashmir returned to Hindu rule, under Rinchan's widow, Kota Rani, but this interlude was but a short one. She was defeated by Shahmir, an astute diplomat in her kingdom, who ascended the throne in 1339 CE, with the title of Sultan Shamsuddin. While Rinchan was the first Muslim ruler of Kashmir, the consolidation of the Sultanate started with Shamsuddin, till the 200 year rule of the Sultans was ended by Mughal emperor Akbar in 1586 CE.

Mughal, Sikh and Dogra Rule

The Mughal rule in Kashmir lasted for just over 170 years until 1757 CE. It was marked by the building of pleasure gardens and little else, till Aurangzeb (1658 CE-1707 CE), ascended the throne. His rule saw the return of religious bigotry and intolerance to the Kashmir Valley, with forcible conversions and discriminatory taxation. Mughal influence declined after Aurangzeb's death, and further weakened after Nadir Shah's invasion of India in 1738 CE. The death knell to Mughal rule came with their defeat to the Afghan's in 1753 CE, as a result of which Kashmir came under Afghan rule. This ended 66 years later with the defeat of the Afghans by Maharaja Ranjit Singh in 1819. This also marked the end of Muslim rule in Kashmir, encompassing a period of just over four hundred years. The Afghan rule was noted for its cruelty, barbarity and avarice, and its demise came as a period of welcome relief to the people of the region.[8]

Sikh rule over Kashmir was also short-lived and ended with British victory over the Sikhs in the battle of Sobraon in February 1846, called the First Anglo-Sikh War. Two treaties were signed at the end of the war. The first of these, the Treaty of Lahore, was signed on 9 March 1846 with the 7-year old Maharaja Duleep Singh and the British Empire. Under the terms of the Treaty, Punjab ceded Kashmir and its dependencies to the British. The second treaty, the Treaty of Amritsar was signed six days later on 13 March 1846 with Maharaja Gulab Singh of Jammu. Through this Treaty, Kashmir and its dependencies were handed over to Gulab Singh, and thus Kashmir came under Dogra rule. Under the terms of the Treaty, Maharaja Gulab Singh paid a sum of Rs 75 lakh to the British government for the territories ceded to him. This included the whole of the outer hills between the Ravi and the Indus, the Valley of Kashmir, Ladakh, Gilgit, Baltistan and the Indus Valley down to Chilas.[9]

The region of modern-day Jammu, was traditionally ruled by the Dogra Rajputs. For the most part, they maintained their autonomy despite being nominal feudatories to Delhi. At times, they joined the Mughals in their northern conquests, like those of Balkh in 1646-47 CE.

With the demise of the Mughal dynasty, Raja Dhruv Deo and later his son, Raja Ranjit Deo rose to greater political prominence, the latter also proceeding to expand his kingdom to include Kishtwar, Chenani, Bhadarwah, Besolhi, Jasrota and parts of Gujrat in Western Punjab. This was, however, a transitory phase as the rise of Sikh power in the region saw Jammu losing its sovereignty over all of their former territories save for Jammu, which was now reduced to a petty state. But it also saw the rise of the line of Raja Dhruv Deo, in the form of his great-great-grandsons, Gulab Singh, Dhian Singh and Suchet Singh, who joined Maharaja Ranjit Singh's court and rose rapidly through the ranks, setting themselves apart and above the Maharaja's Sikh courtiers.

Gulab Singh had joined Maharaja Ranjit Singh's army in 1809. His father, Miyan Kishore Singh was given the charge to administer Jammu state by Maharaja Ranjit Singh in 1817, which had been annexed by him a year earlier. Soon thereafter, Miyan Kishore Singh declared Gulab Singh as his legal heir. As a reward for the outstanding contribution made by Gulab Singh in the defeat of the Pathans in Kashmir in 1819, Maharaja Ranjit Singh crowned Gulab Singh as the Raja of Jammu on 16 June 1822. Even after getting Jammu and its adjoining principalities under his territory, Raja Gulab Singh continued to serve the rulers of Lahore and at the same time, annexed many small principalities to his kingdom. Kishtwar was subdued and its governorship was handed over to Zorawar Singh, a Rajput soldier in the Sikh army. It was Zorawar Singh who annexed Ladakh in 1842 and added it to Dogra rule.[10]

British interest in the region, during the period of Sikh and Dogra rule had much to do with the great power rivalry that existed at that time between Imperial Britain and Czarist Russia. Britain wanted to keep their resident in Kashmir, to keep a watch over the activities of the Sikh rulers and to see that Russian influence was kept at bay. During Maharaja Ranjit Singh's rule and for a decade after his death in June 1839, the British were kept out, but after the defeat of the Sikh's in the Second Anglo-Saxon War of 1849, Punjab was annexed by the British and the Dogra rulers thereafter succumbed to British pressure. In 1877, the British established the Gilgit Agency, to guard against the advance of Russia. The Agency, comprising of the Gilgit Wazarat; the State of Hunza and Nagar; the Punial Jagir; the Governorships of Yasin, Kuh-Ghizr and Ishkoman, and Chilas, was re-established in 1935 under the control of the British Resident in Jammu and Kashmir. It was given on lease for a period of 60 years commencing from 29 March 1935.[11]

The period of Dogra rule in Kashmir's history was an epochal event, for it marked the entry of the British into the area. Taken holistically, it was also a period of reasonable prosperity for the state. Gulab Singh was succeeded by his son Ranbir Singh, who in turn was succeeded by Pratap Singh. Here the family line ended as Pratap Singh had no male heir. As a result, his nephew Hari Singh, succeeded him to the throne. Hari Singh was destined to be the last ruler of the state, the Dogra rule having lasted for just over one hundred years.

Pre-Independence Developments

Maharaja Hari Singh ascended the throne on 23 September 1925. It was a moment in history when the Indian independence movement was gathering steam and differences between the Hindus and Muslims had started coming to the fore. Within the state of J&K, Muslim fanatics started a movement to stoke communal violence in the state.[12] Sheikh Abdullah emerged as the leader of the J&K Muslim Conference which was formed in 1932. The Party was renamed as the Jammu and Kashmir National Conference on 10 June 1939. When India was partitioned and achieved independence on 15 August 1947, most of the princely states had opted to join either India or Pakistan. The state of Jammu and Kashmir had the choice to remain independent under the Maharaja or to join either India or Pakistan. Britain had also terminated its lease of the Gilgit Agency, which reverted back to the state. At this time, the boundaries of the state encompassed the Gilgit Agency, Gilgit and Baltistan in the North, Ladakh in the East, Kashmir and Muzaffarabad in the centre and Jammu, to include Poonch, Rajouri, Mirpur, Udhampur, Bhadarwah and Kathua in the South.

Post-Independence Developments

At the time of independence, Maharaja Hari Singh found himself in a precarious position. His state forces lacked the capacity to protect any part of his landlocked kingdom, which lay between India and Pakistan. There were three battalions of the Jammu and Kashmir State Forces, with the Kashmir Brigade. 7 J&K Rifles was at Srinagar, 4 J&K Rifles at Domel with a company at Kohala and another company at Keran and 6 J&K Battalion had been sent up to Gilgit.

This battalion had moved to Bunji and had a company at Leh and another company at Skardu. South of the Pir Panjal range, 1 J&K Rifles was at Poonch and was being relieved by 8 J&K Rifles, 9 J&K Rifles was at Rawalkot, 2 J&K rifles at Naushera and 3 J&K Rifles at Mirpur.[13] Some of these were mixed battalions with both Dogra and Muslim troops. Poor communications and the vast spread of the area meant that each battalion was really fighting an independent battle and could not depend on support from any one. Pakistan thus thought that it would be easy to militarily take over the state and force its accession to Pakistan.

The idea of remaining an independent kingdom had appeal for the Maharaja, but he lacked the force to protect his kingdom from external threats. The remaining options were to accede, either to India or to Pakistan. Maharaja Hari Singh's dilemma was increased by the fact that the Muslims in his state constituted the larger majority, but the Hindu population was substantial too. Stalling for time, the Maharaja entered into a Standstill Agreement with Pakistan on 12 August 1947. India however declined his offer.

To the Pakistani political leadership of that time, led by Mr Jinnah, who had been appointed as the Governor General of Pakistan and his Prime Minister, Mr Liaquat Ali Khan, there was little doubt that Kashmir would be taken over by force, if the Maharaja did not accede to Pakistan. This plan was given the code name "Operation Gulmarg" and planning commenced in August 1947. Maj Gen Akbar Khan, a serving officer of the Pakistan army, was given the command of Operation Gulmarg, and he revealed all the details of this operation in 1975, in his book, "Raiders in

Kashmir". To achieve their objective, the Pakistan military raised 20 lashkars of about 1000 men each from their Pashtun population in the tribal belt. Pakistani military officers and men were embedded into the lashkars. They were given weapons, equipment and logistic support by the Pakistan army which also provided the force its leadership component down to company level. In his book, Khan confirms that the political leadership of Pakistan was fully in sync with these operations. It was thus a politico-military operation carried out by the state of Pakistan.

The invasion of J&K by Pakistan military, along with the raiders, began on 22 October. The route chosen to reach Srinagar was via Domel, Mahulla and thence to Baramulla. Over 7,000 Pashtun armed tribesmen, led by officers from the Pakistan military, began the invasion, crossing over the state boundary. In a shameful incident, on the night of 21/22 October, the Muslim companies of the 4th Jammu and Kashmir Infantry, betrayed their oath to their ruler and the state and in an act of treachery, driven by religious fanaticism, killed their commanding officer, Col Narain Singh. They also killed their Dogra colleagues and then deserted, crossing over to the ranks of the tribals. Muzaffarabad and Domel was ransacked, the people butchered, raped and looted. Two days later, in Pulandri, they announced the formation of a provisional 'Azad Kashmir' government,[14] before continuing their advance to Srinagar. Under these conditions, the Maharaja requested India's help, but was told that this could not be given unless he acceded to India. This was agreed to by the Maharaja and the Instrument of Accession was signed on 26 October 1947. The Indian Army was flown in to Srinagar on 27 October and the raiders were halted on the outskirts of the city. Thereafter, they were pushed back till a ceasefire was declared on 31 December 1948. With this, Pakistan remained in possession of about one-third of the state of J&K, to include the areas of Gilgit-Baltistan and Mirpur-Muzaffarabad. This line has seen minor modifications post the 1971 war with Pakistan, where it came to be known as the Line of Control. Post the 1971 Indo-Pak War, Turtuk, lying in the Nubra Valley and on the banks of the Shyok River was liberated by Indian forces and now forms one of the northernmost villages in the Leh District of Ladakh.

Article 370

Maharaja Hari Singh remained the titular Maharaja of the state until 1952, when the monarchy was abolished by Government of India, but political power shifted to the National Conference headed by Sheikh Abdullah in 1948 itself. When India's Constitution was promulgated on 26 January 1950, Article 370 was inserted as a temporary Article. The inclusion of Article 370 into the Constitution of India had not been demanded by the people of J&K, nor was it demanded by Maharaja Hari Singh when he acceded to India. The Article, giving special status to the state was a temporary measure, and so was included in PART XXI of the Constitution, which pertained to Temporary, Transitional and Special Provisions. The insertion of Article 35A in 1954, which was a more insidious development, gave the state of J&K the power to determine who was a state subject and such determination could not be challenged by the Indian State. This Article was inserted without the mandatory approval of the Indian Parliament, and thus can be construed as a fraud committed on the Constitution. Both Article 370 and 35 A can be said to have hindered the emotional integration of J&K with the rest of the Indian Union.

The Radicalisation of J&K

The problem of radicalisation which seeped into the state had its origins in the growth, since the mid-1960s, of the Jamaat-e-Islami. Indoctrinated cadres from the Jamaat were soon absorbed in government institutions, particularly in government schools. It was the Jamaat which radicalised the Muslims in J&K, especially in the Valley. The Government banned the Jamaat-e-Islami and its educational wing Falah-e-Aam Trust in 1992 for indulging in anti-social activities, but inexplicably, absorbed all the teachers in government schools![15] Terrorism and radicalisation thus grew hand in hand in J&K, with Pakistan lending full support to terrorist groups. To view the conflict in Kashmir as a fight for 'Azadi', is hence a misnomer. It was always a fight for Nizam-e-Mustafa—rule by Shariat and not by democratic norms. Also, developments with the state always had a Kashmir-centric agenda, despite the Kashmir division having only 55 percent of the population,[16] and just one-sixth of the land area of the state.[17] The voices from Jammu and Ladakh remained smothered. Even within Kashmir Division, it was but a small coterie of people, comprising a fraction of the population, that held complete sway over the state. These were, what Bashir Assad refers to in his book, "K File" as the Mullah clan—the people who had come to the Valley about 600 years earlier to preach Islam. They are the present day Geelanis, Muftis, Shah, Handanis, Naqshbandis, Andrabis, Bukharis etc, and they achieved a stranglehold over the state, dominating the original inhabitants, as well as the states political and bureaucratic landscape.[18] The power of this group has now been eroded. However, the radicalisation which had seeped into Kashmiri society, beginning in the late 1960's, led to the genocide of the Kashmiri Hindus in 1990 and the growth of terrorism in J&K.

Conclusion

The abrogation of Special Status to the state of J&K and its bifurcation into the Union Territory of Jammu and Kashmir (with a legislature) and the Union Territory of Ladakh (without a legislature) on 05 August 2019, brings fresh hope of normalcy settling into the region. The perfidious designs of Pakistan and their supporters within India are finally being addressed, which should bring peace to the region. For the moment, the focus and effort of the government of India remains on seeing the total return to normalcy in the Union Territory of J&K. Elections to the State Assembly are yet to be held, as the work of the Delimitation Commission, proposing changes to assembly and parliamentary segments in the Union Territory, is yet to be finalised and approved. But elections to the local bodies have been successfully held and received tremendous local support. Central laws are now applicable, giving hope to the women, Dalits, West Pakistan Refugees and others who were deprived of their rights and liberties due to the application of Article 370 and 35A. There is also a visible decline in levels of terrorist activities across the state, which bodes well for the future.

Transformative changes however take time, and the challenges are tremendous, especially in ensuring the safe return of the half million or so Kashmiri Hindus back to their homeland. The prospects of total normalcy reverting to J&K are at present, not as bleak as they were prior to 5 August 2019, when the provisions of Article 370 were abrogated, bringing J&K into the national mainstream. Though the road is long, there is hope in the air, especially amongst the youth of the Union Territory.

How is Kashmir seen by youth from other parts of India? Towards that end, a group of young Indians from all over the country visited the UT as part of the India Foundation Young Thinkers Meet held in Kashmir Valley towards the latter half of 2021. Post the conclave, some of the individuals gave out their impressions of the UT and how they view the situation as it is developing. It forms an interesting take on the views of a segment of young India. More such initiatives will result in a better understanding of the horrors of radicalisation and the urgent need to ensure that such movements are nipped in the bud and not allowed to grow.

ENDNOTES

1. This preface is an updated version of an earlier article written by the author, titled 'Jammu and Kashmir: A Glimpse into History,' and is available at https://indiafoundation.in/articles-and-commentaries/jammu-and-kashmir-a-glimpse-into-history/
2. K.S. Valdiya, Geography, People's and Geodynamics of India in Puranas and Epics, A Geologists Interpretation, New Delhi, Aryan Books, 2012, p 33
3. Binod S Das, "The Himalayan Frontier from the Sanskrit Sources" in N.R. Ray, Editor, Himalayan Frontier in Historical Perspective, Calcutta, Institute of Historical Studies, 1986, p. 2.
4. The Discovery of India, pp. 49-52.
5. K. Sadeswin, "The Himalayas in early Tamil Literature" in N.R. Ray, Editor, Himalaya Frontier in Historical Perspective, Institute of Historical Studies, Calcutta, 1986, p. 8.

6	EA Paemu, A History of Muslim Rule in Kashmir, 1320-1819, Chapter 3, available at https:// archive.org/stream/in.ernet.dli.2015.118667/2015.118667.A-History-Of-Muslim-Rule-In-Kashmir_djvu.txt
7	Mohammad Ashraf, Shah-i-Hamadan, the "Apostle of Kashmir", Kashmir First, available at http://www.kashmirfirst.com/articles/history/070520_shah-i-hamadan.htm, accessed on 2 December 2019.
8	Arjan Nath Chaku & Inder K Chaku, The Kashmir Story through the ages, Vitasta Publishing, New Delhi, p. 3.
9	Ibid.
10	Note 7, pp. 21-26.
11	Note 7, pp. 27-28.
12	Note 7, p. 49.
13	Rohit Singh, Operations in Jammu and Kashmir, 1947-48, Scholar Warrior, Autumn 2012, available at https://archive.claws.in/images/journals_doc/SW%20i-10.10.2012.150-178.pdf
14	Verghese Koithara, Crafting Peace in Kashmir through a Realist Lens, Sage, New Delhi, p. 38.
15	Bashir Assad, K File: The Conspiracy of Silence, Vitasta, New Delhi, pp. 36-39.
16	Census of India, 2011.
17	This does not include territories illegally occupied by China and Pakistan.
18	Bashir Assad, p. 2-18.

Contributors

Major General Dhruv C. Katoch served as the Director of the Indian Army's Think Tank, Centre for Land Warfare Studies till Nov 2014. A third generation army officer, he has been awarded the degree of Doctor of Philosophy (honoris Causa) from the Indira Gandhi University, Rewari in 2016. Presently, he is Director, India Foundation, Editor, SALUTE Magazine and Secretary General, Indian War Veterans Association.

Aaditya Tiwari is currently working as Officer on Special Duty to the Chief Minister of Arunachal Pradesh Shri Pema Khandu. He is also a Visiting Fellow with India Foundation. Aaditya had assisted then Member of Parliament from Rajya Sabha Shri Swapan Dasgupta in his research. He has previously worked as a Fellow with Teach For India, where he taught in a low income school teaching primary class students for two years. He completed his engineering in Chemical Technology from Harcourt Butler Technological Institute, Kanpur where he interned with Hindustan Unilever. He has authored two chapters in the book 'Public Policy: A Citizen's Guide' and written articles for platforms like Press Information Bureau, Government of India, Indian Express, Firstpost and weekly magazine Organiser.

Soumya Chaturvedi is an International Relations scholar. A lawyer by education, she holds a postgraduate degree in Diplomacy and an additional specialization in Asia Pacific Security. Her research areas include geo-politics and geo-economics of South Asia, India's internal security, amongst others. Since August 2019, she was steering the Jammu and Kashmir Security Tracker Project as a part of her endeavours to contribute towards counter-terrorism studies in India. Previously she was a Senior Research Fellow at India Foundation. Currently, she is a Consultant at the G20 Secretariat, Ministry of External Affairs, India.

Ajit Datta is an author and political commentator. He is the biographer of Assam's Chief Minister Dr. Himanta Biswa Sarma, and has columns in several publications. He is one of the voices behind The Frustrated Indian, and has co-founded one of India's foremost literature festivals, the Pondy Lit Fest.

Dhairya Roy is a senior Corporate Affairs, Consulting and Marketing professional with 15 years of team leading experience in the Government sector, Corporate sector and the Media & Entertainment sector. He is the alumnus of Columbia Business School, New York University, NYU Wagner & Oxford University, Said Business school. He specialises in leading big ticket government projects, implementing change management processes in public policies, executing 360-degree marketing campaigns and raising funds for Government projects. He has been a part of award-winning campaigns like 500 Million Plantation Drive, Green Army, River Rejuvenation and Mudra Banking. He has led the team which received appreciation from the

Prime Minister of India for their marketing campaign on environment conservation. Dhairya led the change management process in the Ministry of Finance which enabled the project execution rates to jump from 30% to 84 % for 101 projects. Dhairya has also marketed and distributed 63 films in the international markets. 3 of these films were nominated for the Academy Awards.

Hamsa Devineni is a practicing lawyer in Hyderabad and holds an LLM distinction in Admiralty & Maritime laws from Tulane University, USA. She is a visiting faculty at NALSAR, Hyderabad and NALANDA University, Rajgir and was previously a visiting fellow at the National Maritime Foundation, New Delhi. She is also a politician and has served as the spokesperson of BJP Andhra Pradesh and contested as the BJP Lok Sabha candidate for Ananthapur constituency in the 2019 General Elections.

Abhishek Malhotra is currently working as a Consultant with the office of Chief Economic Adviser, Ministry of Finance, Government of India. He is pursuing Ph.D. in Economics from University of Hyderabad specialising in the field of Urban Economics and Infrastructure Financing. He was earlier associated with Indian Institute of Management, Ahmedabad (IIM-A) as a Research Associate. He has published several research papers in national and international journals. He actively contributes articles for various magazines and news portals. Abhishek is a member of the Central Executive Committee of World Organisation of Students and Youth (WOSY).

Nidhi Vyas is a practicing advocate at Gujarat High Court, Ahmedabad. She graduated with an honors degree in Law with two gold medals in Arbitration Law & Taxation law and holds a Master degree in Business Law from Maharaja Sayajirao University of Baroda. She also has a diploma in cyber law from Gujarat Law Society, Mumbai. She is currently Assistant Government Pleader in Gujarat High Court representing the State of Gujarat in various land, service, education, election, constitutional and policy related matters.

Sammridh Varma is an alumnus of University of California Los Angeles and Cambridge institute of Sustainable leadership. He is a member of BJP Bihar and currently associated with Bihar Young Thinkers Forum.

Dr. Abhishek Pratap Singh holds PhD in Chinese Studies from JNU and is Faculty, Deshbandhu College, University of Delhi. He was Fellow, South Asia Democratic Forum (SADF), Brussels and also Visiting Scholar, Centre for India Studies, Shenzhen University, China. He is also a member of the Hindi Advisory Committee, NITI Aayog under Government of India.

Dr. Aakansha Bhawsar, former scientist, ICMR Headquarters, New Delhi, India.

Ujjwal Virendra Deepak has served as OSD to the Former Chief Minister of Chhattisgarh, Dr Raman Singh. An alumnus of Columbia University, USA, he is currently the President of Chhattisgarh Young Thinkers Forum.

Ashutosh Dubey, an electronics engineer by education and a poet by passion, served as a parliamentary assistant to Loksabha member,Shri Abhishek singh ji for five years and was part of Strategy-Media team of Ex CM Chhatisgarh,Dr Raman singh ji. He is currently serving as a member of state executive committee,BJYM Chhatisgarh.

Mishika Nayyar is a research specialist in the field of public policy and foreign investments and is currently working with Invest India as part of the Strategic Investment Research Unit (SIRU), the internal think-tank of Invest India. She has published over 20 research reports showcasing myriad opportunities for FDI inflow in the Indian economy. Having a demonstrated history of working across governments, corporates and development agencies, she has been a Kautilya Fellow, a fellowship programme designed by India Foundation and Ministry of External Affairs, Government of India and has been invited by the Ministry of Foreign Affairs, Government of Greece to represent India on an international cultural delegation. An oral historian by passion, she has published her papers on the 1947 Partition in South Asia across journals and has been invited by Oral History Society to present her research findings from 60 partition survivors at University of Leeds, UK. Mishika Nayyar is an alumna of Lady Shri Ram College for Women, University of Delhi and Centre for Historical Studies, Jawaharlal Nehru University.

Swayam Prakash Baral is a first-generation entrepreneur who began his entrepreneurial journey at the age of 23 after completing his education at University of Stirling, UK. His current entrepreneurial engagements are in the field of Renewable Energy, Event Management, Agriculture, IT & Manpower. Swayam is also a Trustee of 'Youth for Seva', a national level social organization working to engage the youth in various volunteering activities. He oversees the "Clean Tech Initiative" program of Sewa International which is a global charitable organization having branches in many countries around the world. Swayam's work has been recognized in the field of entrepreneurship and social work and he is the recipient of the prestigious "National Youth Leadership Award - 2018" for his extraordinary achievements.

Chiranjeevi Bhat is a journalist at Hosa Digantha Kannada daily. He has previously worked in Vishwavaani, Kannada Prabha, Suvarna News 24/7 and Samaya News. He mainly focuses on defense, security, politics, distortion and appropriation.

Aparajita Tripathi is an engineer and an alumnus of IIM Kozhikode and works as Director, KPMG. She enjoys reading, writing, and a cup of chai while watching rain.

1

TEN YEARS OF THE YOUNG THINKERS MEET (YTM)

Aaditya Tiwari

A decade long journey for an institution or an event that marks an important milestone is the time to look back and reflect on the path it has trudged. Young Thinkers Meet (YTM) is one such initiative of the India Foundation that began its journey in 2012 at Coorg, Karnataka, and recently concluded its tenth edition in Pahalgam, Jammu & Kashmir. The annually held event has become a confluence of young nationalistic minds hailing from varied walks of life across India.

To give it some context, YTM is an annual get-together organised by the New Delhi based think tank, India Foundation, for individuals *(mostly under 35 years)* who are driven by the idea of a New India. YTM today has an alumni base of over three hundred individuals who belong to different parts of India and come with unique life experiences and skill sets. There are social activists, political activists, NGO workers, academics, journalists, scientists, corporate professionals and students from reputed national and international universities. Participants in the YTM come from all parts of the country and deliberate and debate on issues of contemporary national importance. The format of the meet is immersive and experiential rather than a lecture-based classroom format. The number of delegates at any YTM has varied from seventy-five to eighty-five and involve freewheeling discussion over two to three days. Each year, YTM moves to a new location and helps the young delegates explore the incredible diversity of the country. The Meet has previously been held in Coorg, Karnataka; Manesar, Haryana; Pune, Maharashtra; Panchmarhi, Madhya Pradesh; Patni Top, J&K; Vadodara, Gujarat; Kasauli, Himachal Pradesh; Chilika, Odisha and this year it was held in Pahalgam and Srinagar, J&K. Due to the national lockdown, YTM was organised virtually in 2020.

The various themes of the YTM have been the 'Great Indian Dream', 'Impacting the National Discourse', 'India-2047', 'New Age Leadership', 'New India—Ideas, Concepts and Contestations', and 'Know Kashmir'. In 2020, a day long working group meeting for select YTM alumni was held to discuss 'Indian Democracy@2030'. Inspired by the idea of the Thinkers Meet, many alumni have started regional chapters of the YTM, following the format of the national event. As of today, there are active chapters in the states of Tamil Nadu, Gujarat, Karnataka, Bihar, Uttar Pradesh, Uttarakhand, Madhya Pradesh and Chhattisgarh, led by enterprising and visionary young minds.

I have been a delegate and part of the organising committee of the YTM since 2013 and have been a witness to the strength of this community that has evolved much like a family. There are three primary types of learning that I feel must be shared for similar initiatives that wish to work for the country and would benefit from our extensive experience:

In my informal conversations with the delegates and alumni of the YTM, I have realised a common strain and that is the power of *mentorship*. Participants across the years have shared how Shri Ram Madhav, the visionary and driving force of this idea, has been a constant guide and mentor to them through the years. Always approachable and generous with his insights, he has guided many to think deeply about their work and scale it in terms of vision and execution. For youngsters to be able to find someone who can show them a broad long-term view vis-a-vis immediate short-term gains is a great treasure and every participant at the YTM has benefitted from this.

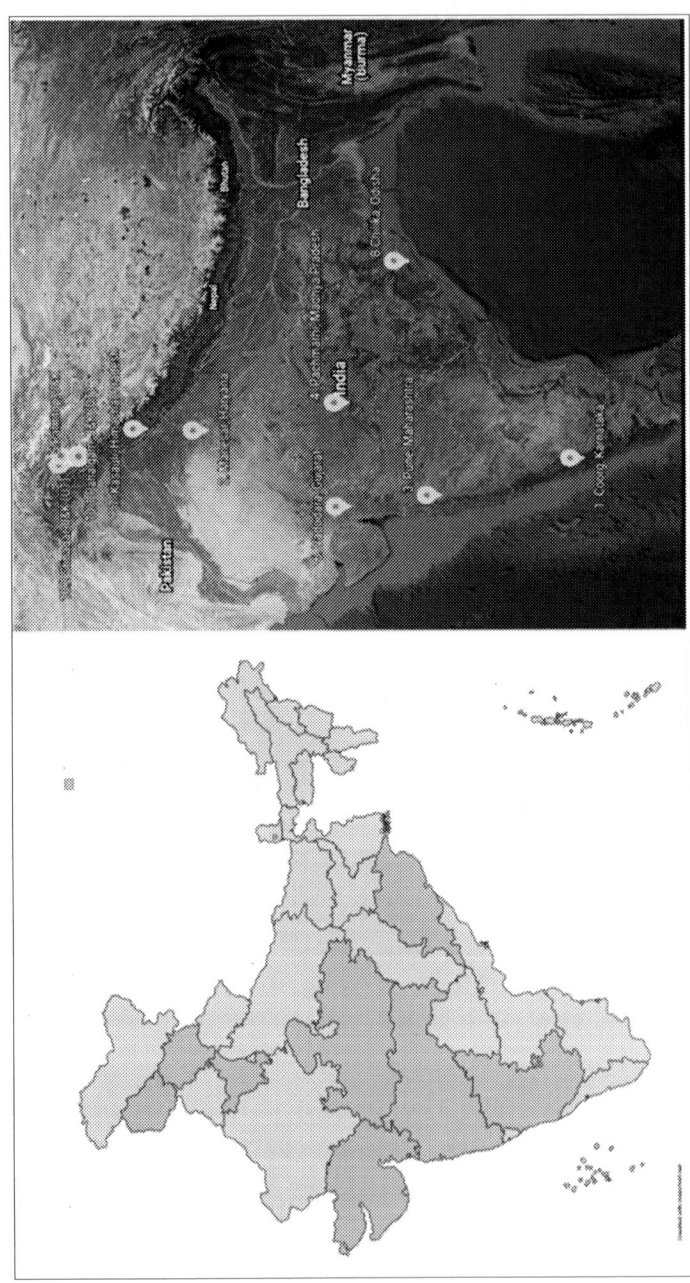

YTM has allowed delegates to express their views and share their ideas *freely*. There are no restrictions to what one says so long as it is said respectfully and without hurting sentiments. This has expanded the vision of the participants and helped them view issues beyond binaries. The delegates come from all corners of the country and have their own understanding of various issues. To be able to listen, process and realise such a perspective is a unique opportunity for young minds.

National interest is foremost and young minds should involve themselves in working towards the growth and progress of India. This is the message all delegates leave YTM with. There may be heated discussions or disagreements on particular issues but the strength of YTM is to bring together youngsters who believe in India and are ready to sacrifice their self interest for the sake of the nation. To find so many youngsters working in their own silos on one platform and bind them in a network is rare and inspirational.

YTM has evolved as a platform for collaboration and exchange of ideas. Many alumni of YTM are today Members of Parliament, hold senior positions in national political parties, and are leading entrepreneurs, senior public policy professionals, corporate leaders, columnists in leading newspapers, media panellists and authors of several books. YTM has exposed its alumni to leading public intellectuals at a nascent career stage and has helped them chart their paths. Many alumni worked together during the COVID-19 crisis to help the under-served and could do this because of their friendships and informal networks of like-minded individuals across the country. The YTM network has become an inextricable part of the lives of those who have participated in it and continue to cherish lifelong memories and friendships forged in the days of the Meet. The past decade has been a wonderful journey; the next would surely be an exciting and promising one.

2

EVOLVING SECURITY DYNAMICS OF J&K

Soumya Chaturvedi

There was a time when any conversation on Jammu & Kashmir (J&K) was perceived to be flirting around its pristine beauty, despite contested borders, occupied lands and having hosted wars between three nuclear powers—India, Pakistan, and China. However, the fate of J&K dramatically altered in the 1990s. Islamabad and Rawalpindi succeeded in their agenda of radicalising the local population of J&K, and inciting them to resort to violence while providing all kinds of material and non-material support. J&K became the hub of terrorism in India, hosting outfits with separatist and radical Islamic *jihadi* ideologies. The Valley was burning, and the result was the brutal exodus of thousands of Kashmiri Hindus, forcing them to live as refugees in their own country. This one event changed the socio-cultural, political, and economic fabric of J&K and caused irreparable damage for decades to come. Henceforth, the discussions and conversations on J&K were perceived to be navigating around its security scenario.

While the security situation in J&K would witness seasons of peace and an increase in violence for the years to follow, the negative perceptions and stereotypes about J&K became deeply ingrained in the Indian psyche. Over the years, the Indian security architecture succeeded in controlling the security scenario and limiting the terrorist battlefields, but the larger perception remained that J&K continues to burn. Occasional episodes of Burhan Wani and terrorist attacks overshadowed the efforts of the Indian security forces in normalising the situation. The local politicians would often take advantage of this for their own benefit and ensure that *'dilli se dil ki duri'* sustains. On August 5, 2019, the Indian government abrogated the special status of J&K through parliamentary action. The government's intent was clear that misuse of Art. 370, a temporary provision in the Constitution, had to be done away with to ensure the welfare of the people of J&K and remove the last obstacle in the emotional integration of the region with the rest of the country. While this action had several political ramifications, looking at through the lens of security, two arguments were advocated in the corridors of New Delhi. First, the decision will ensure greater focus by the Central Government on security and development. This, coupled with a lack of local political interference, will ensure a drastic reduction in terrorism-related violence and, thus, lead to an improvement in the security scenario. Second, masterminds sitting in Islamabad and Rawalpindi will capitalise on this opportunity and increase terrorism-related violence in J&K

to register the illusionary discontentment of the local population against Parliament's decision.

While proving or disapproving both the arguments would require a rigorous analysis of several factors, it was essential to monitor the security developments in J&K. To gather independent data and analyse the trends, the J&K Security Tracker Project was curated. The project analyses the physical manifestation of violence by non-state and foreign actors in J&K and quantifies verticals such as encounters, arrests of terrorists, unprovoked ceasefire violations, etc. It provides incident-wise, district-wise and terrorist outfit-wise analysis.

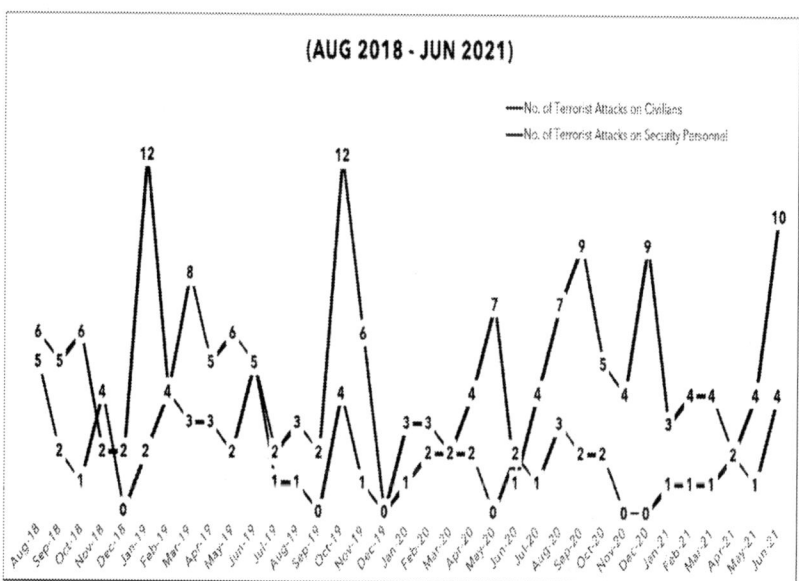

Figure 1: Graph depicting the trend of terrorist attacks aimed at civilians and security personnel in J&K between August 2018 and June 2021. The data has been taken from multiple reports published under the J&K Security Tracker Project available at https://indiafoundation.in/category/report/

Data collected between August 2018 and June 2021 was studied. The graph of the total number of attacks is primarily a combination of crests and troughs (Figure 1). However, a considerable decline is seen in attacks on civilians and a slight increase in the attacks on security personnel. The attacks on civilians have largely been targeted political assassinations. While being low in 2019, the attacks on security personnel appears to have increased considerably in 2020 and 2021.

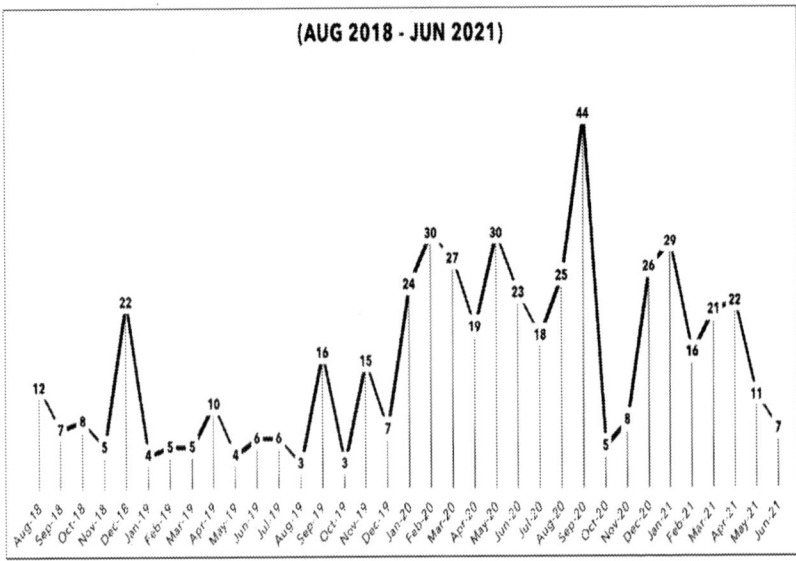

Figure 2: Graph depicting the trend of terrorists arrested in J&K between August 2018 and June 2021. The data has been taken from multiple reports published under the J&K Security Tracker Project available at https://indiafoundation.in/category/report/

Since September 2019, a significant increase was observed in the number of terrorists arrested (Figure 2). Apart from active terrorists, these included several fresh recruits and overground workers (OGWs). On the other hand, the graph indicating the number of terrorists neutralised has a slight

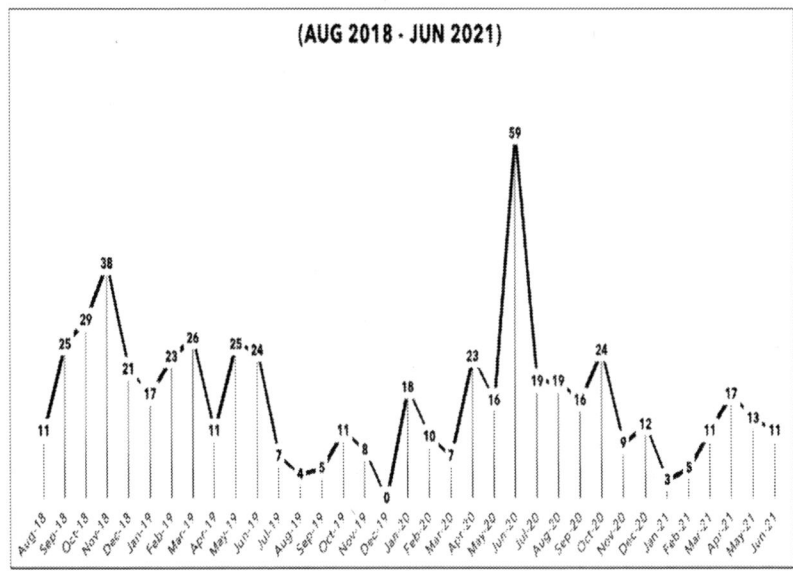

Figure 3: *Graph depicting the trend of terrorists neutralised in J&K between August 2018 and June 2021. The data has been taken from multiple reports published under the J&K Security Tracker Project available at https://indiafoundation.in/category/report/*

downward slope (Figure 3). When both the graphs are analysed together, it is evident that more terrorists have been arrested than killed. It implies two things—first, with more arrests, the security forces have a chance to interrogate terrorists and gather more intelligence or corroborate the existing findings. It can be verified from the increased elimination of terrorist hideouts in J&K and, more importantly, unearthing of tunnels used for smuggling arms, ammunition, and terrorists into Jammu, Kathua and Samba districts. Second, the forces can arrest with better intelligence and planning while ensuring that encounters or firings do not break out.

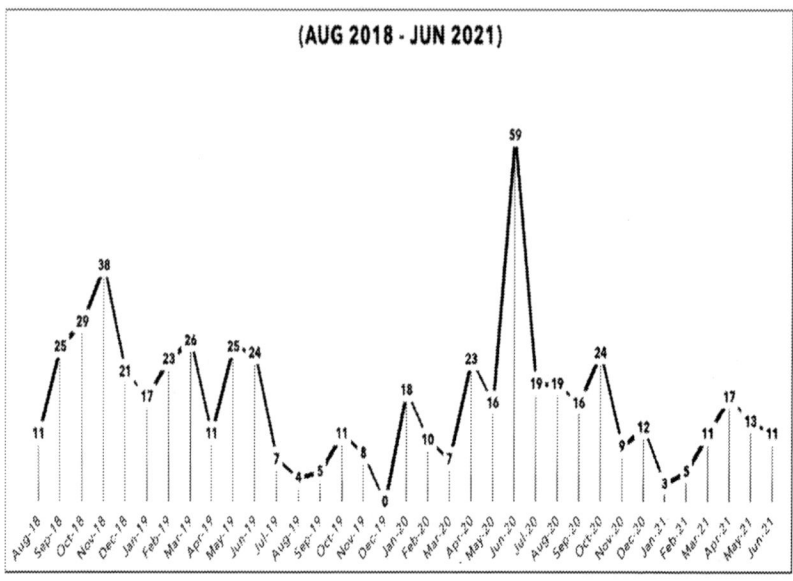

Figure 4: Graph depicting the number of days in the month unprovoked ceasefire violations were initiated by Pakistan in J&K between August 2018 and June 2021. The data has been taken from multiple reports published under the J&K Security Tracker Project available at https://indiafoundation.in/category/report/.

Another interesting trend was observed in ceasefire violations. In the aftermath of the abrogation of the special status of J&K, an unprecedented surge in unprovoked ceasefire violations by Pakistan was observed. It resulted in considerably high civilian casualties and the destruction of civilian infrastructure. In February 2021, after the agreement between the militaries of both countries to observe the Ceasefire Pact of 2003, the violations stopped barring one day of such violations in Samba district.

It is also imperative to note the developments in J&K (UT) when a significant portion of military personnel and intelligence was involved in the Ladakh standoff against China. In June 2020, when the Ladakh standoff was at its peak, there were 24 days of unprovoked ceasefire violations by Pakistan, 59 terrorists were neutralised, and 23 were arrested by Indian security forces in different districts of J&K. This would mean that while a significant proportion of Indian security architecture was busy looking eastwards handling China, there was another part handling Pakistan at the borders a few hundred kilometres to the west and terrorism within J&K. Due to the pandemic, a part was also involved in maintaining the law-and-order situation in J&K. This one incident is evidence enough to highlight not just the magnanimity of the Indian security Architecture, but also the strategic depth that ensured that the national security of India does not succumb to any threat or adversary.

It is needless to restate the improving security scenario of J&K. However, it is essential to visit the factors that may challenge this improvement. One such factor is the Taliban-Afghanistan conundrum. The Taliban's affiliation with terrorist groups like al-Qaeda, Haqqani network, Jaish-e-Mohammed, etc., is well known. With the Talibani foothold increasing in Afghanistan, there is a fear that recruitment and training of terrorists from Jaish-e-Mohammed and its affiliates such as Lashkar-e-Mustafa may witness an enhanced focus. Another concern emanating from this would be the animosity between Taliban and Islamic State-Khorasan. While there have already been violent encounters between the two in Afghanistan, there is a fear that this animosity may spill over in J&K between Jaish and Islamic State (IS) presence in India along with outfits such as Lashkar-e-Taiba, which is ideologically closer to IS.

Another challenge is posed by technological and warfare advancements. In the June 2021 attack on the Jammu airbase, there is a possibility that drones were used for the attack. Several suspicious drone activities have already been witnessed across Jammu, Kathua, Poonch, and Samba districts. With more concentrated development flowing into J&K, there will be a considerable threat to critical state infrastructure.

If the past few years hold any testimony to the strength of the Indian security forces and establishment, then it is evident that they have stood tall and strong against any threat to India's national security. It was seen in J&K too. However, the closer J&K society moves towards normalcy, the more renewed attempts will be made by anti-India forces to bring back fear and terror in the people's minds. India must pre-empt the threats and challenges for J&K and be proactive in its strategic thought and planning.

3

REFLECTIONS ON KASHMIR

Ajit Datta

Dal Lake, Srinagar

India Foundation hosted the tenth edition of the Young Thinkers Meet at Pahalgam and Srinagar in the Kashmir Valley. The forum intended to enable interaction with various stakeholders from the region and enhance the understanding of the region's social and political realities. We interacted with people at different levels, representing different viewpoints, some of whom told us exactly what we wanted to hear, while some others told us just the opposite. Still, others quietly pushed what we did not want to hear, carefully couched in terms that we like to hear. These interactions shattered many of our preconceived notions about Kashmir. However, every new perspective, instead of progressively adding a new shade to our understanding, made the complete picture increasingly elusive. It is evident that the region's political and social realities cannot be defined in a homogenous or straightforward manner. This article is an attempt to highlight the many perspectives that we were exposed to in the Valley, to gain a semblance of clarity about the multilayered complexities that were laid out to us.

Historically, the political class of Kashmir was dominated by two family-run parties. These parties were largely dependent on votes from the Valley, and therefore, had allowed for the continuation of the disproportionate electoral influence of the region. They had split personalities; back in Delhi they swore allegiance to India, while on the ground, they encouraged anti-India sentiment. Their primary election plank had been that New Delhi was seeking to abrogate Article 370, which supposedly provided benefits to the people of the state. They claimed to be the only bulwark against such a move, promising the people that Article 370 would never be abrogated as long as their reign continued.

The commitment to Article 370, however, seems to have stemmed not from an ideological or fundamentalist standpoint, but from a transactional one. Large sums of money that New Delhi had poured into the state, flowed into an elaborate patronage network fostered by both parties. Lakhs of people and their entire families have been dependent on the government and the security forces for employment. Similarly, a large section of the youth has been on the payroll of entities attempting to destabilise the Valley. Essentially, it was important for the conflict to continue, since many livelihoods depended on it. Having Article 370 as the central political plank was necessary at multiple levels to uphold the status quo. Its presence in the political discourse encouraged an anti-India undercurrent. It never allowed the Indian state to have as strong a footing as in other parts of India, forcing it to compensate with a bloated state apparatus. And in turn, these factors allowed anti-India forces to operate, neatly balancing a fragile ecosystem. The political class was happy to allow separatist and fundamentalist forces to operate as long as things did not get too out of hand, and it was happy to allow New Delhi to carry out its agenda as long as their powers remained unaffected. The media's role here must be noted as well since it played an important part in perpetuating the conflict, many a time making mountains out of molehills. Militancy in the state affected a handful of districts, and the number of militants was in hundreds. It was never a Taliban or an ISIS-like situation involving hordes of people. The media, however, gave the world a different picture. As someone in the security establishment pointed out to us, Srinagar's Lal Chowk was never the most volatile point in the conflict yet most attacks were perpetrated here simply because the media outlets were stationed nearby to dutifully provide the desired coverage. Even the occasional stone-pelting and raising of ISIS flags here were orchestrated for optimal coverage.

However, large parts of the population remained outside this ecosystem or the patronage networks. Politically, several options other than the dominant parties existed as well, with strong constituencies. The Congress Party too had always maintained a foothold in the region, including when it was considered as the Indian nationalist representative on the Valley's political spectrum. Of late, the BJP has made steady inroads in Jammu and Ladakh and has become less untouchable amongst the Valley's political class. The biggest testament to this was the 2015 post-poll BJP-PDP alliance government. As a senior politician brought to our notice, he had sought votes in the name of PM Narendra Modi and managed to win the second-highest vote share in the Valley. Trends indicate that in the years leading to the abrogation of Article 370, the electoral fortunes of both the family-run parties were already on the decline.

Another interesting point that a politician from the Valley made was that the death of Burhan Wani saw higher levels of mobilisation and violence than the abrogation of Article 370. When it was finally abrogated, nothing really happened. The conflict and the article supporting it had benefited only a handful of people, and the majority of the population was barely impacted. Perhaps that is why the common man had lost interest in demanding it. Today, despite heavy militarisation and the security apparatus enjoying a freer hand, the administration is leaving no stone unturned to take development to the last man in the queue. Elected representatives in local bodies tell us that due to the generous financial packages from New Delhi, they have more money than they can spend. Notwithstanding the pandemic, tourism is flourishing like never before. The scope for investment and growth is at an all-time high. New Delhi seems to have empowered a new political class at the grassroots and is making attempts to uplift the common man. Linking the assembly elections to the delimitation exercise is also a clever card that New Delhi has played.

Yet, several questions remain unanswered. The first and foremost is the extent to which de-radicalisation can occur under the present circumstances. A Kashmiri we met while trekking in Pahalgam told us, "We are experts in telling you what you want to hear". Will this transactional mindset benefit New Delhi's development-oriented approach? What is it really that the common Kashmiri seeks? Fundamentalist elements exist in the Valley, and across the border, ready to exploit every fault line. New Delhi will have to tread carefully. Dismantling the double-faced political class was only a first step. Another interesting insight that we came across was that even lower-middle-class families in the Valley are more landed and inherently better off than their counterparts across the country. A steady income has enabled many youngsters to remain idle. How would you convince such people to take part in the Valley's growth story? This too shall be a challenge, since young idle minds in the Valley are not in anyone's best interests.

Some pertinent questions about the new political class in the Valley remain unanswered. New political parties have formed and are gaining traction there, replacing the old guard. For new parties led by leaders like Sajad Lone (Jammu and Kashmir People's Conference) and Altaf Bukhari (Jammu and Kashmir Apni Party), post August 5, 2019, Jammu and Kashmir, without any special status or autonomy, is a reality. The Gupkar Alliance has been forced to accept this new reality. At the local level, newly elected representatives seem full of hope for the future, and full of praise for New Delhi and its proactive approach. At the leadership level, however, questions persist. These leaders have been part of the erstwhile political class of the Valley, patronage networks and even separatist circles. More than whether the new setup can take them along, will they be able to function within it and guide it in the state? The clamour for the restoration of statehood has already begun. New Delhi will have to be mindful of pitfalls while dealing with the issue of statehood, and in its interactions with the new political class.

The key takeaway is that there is a lot more than what meets the eye. Political or media narratives can mislead the beholder. Various stakeholders must be continuously engaged to get a better perspective of the ground realities. Although it might be too soon to say, I am hoping that what we saw were glimmers of a bold new beginning.

4

MY TRYST WITH KASHMIR POST THE ABROGATION OF ARTICLE 370

Dhairya Roy

An invitation to the Young Thinkers Meet (YTM) in Kashmir was a very alluring proposition for various reasons: (a) I had never visited Kashmir before; (b) I would get to interact with the who's who of Kashmir (stakeholders across political platforms); and (c) Young thinkers' forum had over 50 participants with versatile profiles (from researchers, media personnel, corporate professionals, and young budding politicians to novelists and many more).

A perfect semi-paid working holiday (networking with a fun element). When I reached Kashmir, I tried doing what everyone tries doing in such meets, putting on a phony pseudo-intellectual façade, perhaps the best way to leave an impression. A bus ride from Srinagar to Pahalgam eased my tension. My intellectual makeup was perhaps washed away with water and my usual sarcasm followed. As soon as we reached Pahalgam, I found that I had to share a room with one of the participants. Now my paranoia was playing tricks with me. How will I manage this? Sharing a bathroom? Fighting over TV? I thought the horror had just started. I was so wrong. The next three days would teach me my life's biggest lesson—being open to new ideas, new lessons and enjoying the process of life.

A Group Photo at the Young Thinkers Meet.

My newfound openness was perhaps my best tool to assimilate the experience of Kashmir. My ideology has always been clear, a patriotic Indian, a liberal Hindu who is proud of his Indianness. I can proudly say India has 19,500 languages/dialects and 10+ religions. Show me one country in the world that has such diversity. One image/video that I had in my mind about Kashmir was the 2014-2015 floods when stones were pelted at the army while they were trying to rescue flood victims. I was perplexed; why would someone hate their own army so much? Was this a general feeling or an aberration? Was the youth radicalised or misguided? Was the media amplifying the hatred?

I realised one thing; Kashmir essentially had three kinds of ideologies: (1) nationalistic; (2) radicalised; and (3) confused. The nationalistic ideology is clear; we are all one. Why does any state need special treatment? The radical ideology bordered on separatism and religious fanaticism. The most intriguing ideology was the third set of people, the confused set. Who were these people? What were their views on Article 370, 35A? Were they anti-India?

In three days, the young participants of YTM heard close to eight politicians in mainstream Kashmir (across all ideologies), 15 presentations, five panel discussions, IAS officers, IPS officers, Constitutional representatives like the Lt Governor; followed by a mock debate (parliament-style role play). This stirring of ideas was a great way to form our own opinions. It was neither suggestive nor coercive. It was independent irrespective of ideologies.

I observed that Kashmir just was not nationalism vs separatism. It produced different types of ideology sets. Local politicians were caught in a battle of political survival. *'Abolishment of Article 370, 35A and announcement of Jammu & Kashmir as a Union Territory has taken all our power away'*, thundered a local political leader. *'Bureaucracy doesn't listen to us anymore; this is so insulting. Give us our state back. Why do we have to prove our patriotism towards India everyday'*. Local leaders spoke in a similar tone, 5 August 2019 had changed everything. The leaders no longer spoke about 370 and 35A. They just wanted statehood back. Leaders might still raise these issues for political posturing but in their minds, they know, this is an irreversible decision. Soft nationalism is the new normal in Kashmir, even for political leaders. Two years after the abrogation of Article 370 we saw the Indian flag all over Dal Lake. This is something to be proud of.

I found a commonality between the political class in Delhi and the bureaucracy. They are on the same page. They want to prove that they have solved an age-old legacy issue of integrating Kashmir with India. The Lt Governor is on a time-bound mission in Jammu and Kashmir fully supported by the bureaucracy, He wants to prove a point in administration and implement impossible projects like BEAMs (Budget estimation and monitoring system) which took years to implement in other states, but was miraculously implemented in Kashmir in four months.

Two years after the historical abrogation of Article 370:

- The J&K government has issued 41.05 lakh Domicile Certificates;
- 890 Central laws have been made applicable to J&K;
- 205 J&K state laws have been repealed, and
- 130 state laws have been modified and applied in J&K.

The youth of Kashmir is the most difficult to read. Most of them did not care about 370 and 35A when I spoke to them. What they were worried about was the legitimacy of their state. "When will we be a state? Will we ever be one? Why this stepmotherly treatment? Will Delhi control us?" Nobody was discussing Article 370. This is perhaps because they knew the Government would never ever reverse this decision. Whatever be the case, I strongly believe in one thing: that 370 and 35A is an event of the past. Modi-Shah have successfully started a new chapter in Kashmir's future, a chapter of positive nationalism.

This article was first published in the Sunday Guardian.

5

Knowing Kashmir and Kashmiris

Hamsa Devineni

Jammu & Kashmir, for a common man in India, evokes varied thoughts. From its resplendent natural beauty of snow-capped Himalayan peaks, crystal clear lakes and rivers to a place that houses sacred Hindu temples like Vaishno Devi and Amarnath, Kashmir is also known as a place brutalised by constant violence, stone-pelting, grenade attacks, terrorism, insurgency, missing children, wailing mothers and heavily armed security personnel constantly guarding homes and streets.

Today, while the mainstream national newspapers carry at least one news item every week pertaining to Jammu & Kashmir, most of which relate to terror incidents or terror outfits, the social media and Internet sources consistently assure tourists that it is safe to stay and travel in J&K. A recent trip to Kashmir enabled interactions with local Kashmiris, security forces, administrative officials, the region's political leaders, journalists, former militants, and the J&K police, giving an all-new perspective of the region and its people.

Kashmir cannot be understood without its history. When India attained independence from the British in 1947 and separated from Pakistan on a religious basis, J&K was a major bone of contention for both India and Pakistan. While Pakistan claimed that J&K must join the Muslim majority Pakistan being the only remaining Muslim majority state, India claimed J&K belonged to it, as J&K was primarily a Hindu state. Owing to the misdeeds of our erstwhile leaders, J&K joined the Indian Union, albeit, as an independent and autonomous state with its exclusive constitution, exclusive laws, an exclusive flag and exclusive resident rights for its people, different from the rest of India. For India it was a state with special privileges while Pakistan believed that the autonomous state would soon accede to Pakistan. This confused and ill-conceived accession of J&K had led to the perpetual alienation of the Kashmiris from the rest of the Indians, which was skilfully exploited, by Pakistan, as well as the separatists and terror outfits, to sustain violence in the region, which most often, also, spilt over to almost all parts of India.

This forced New Delhi to deploy heavily armed security personnel tasking them with containing the violence with no thought or strategy to address J&K's root problem, i.e., its constitutional autonomy that led to the alienation of its people from the rest of the country and Pakistan's territorial claims to J&K with its consistent and disruptive interference in the affairs of the state. As a result, the people of J&K became perpetually confused, anxious and alienated with constant fear of losing a loved one to either the terrorists or the security personnel and due to the state's constitutional autonomy and exclusivity, they were constrained from seeking any assistance or shelter from New Delhi. India needs J& K and its residents not only for its Switzerland-like terrain and weather or because it historically belonged to us, but because its people have in their hearts believed in the idea of India and surrendered to the Indian Union 74 years ago, very much like many princely states and their people.

Today, although India geographically administers most of J&K's territory and the abrogation of Article 370 has led to the constitutional and administrative integration of J&K with the rest of India, most residents of J&K are still confused and anxious with uncertainty looming large in their hearts and minds. With innocence in their blood, their experiences have taught them survival skills, which is evident by their innocent and tactful conversations. Economically, although the state receives hefty grants from the Central Government, its people primarily depend on agriculture and tourism, both of which still have a huge potential for improvement. While the public sector remains a major source of employment for young Kashmiris, what the people of J&K need is not employment or development alone, for an average Kashmiri owns a four to six bedroom-villa with a backyard comprising walnut and apple trees, enough to give the family an above middle class standard of life. The people of J&K seek employment generation and development from the government, more to keep their young ones away from the pressures and influence of anti-national elements and not merely for their economic sustenance.

Though J&K's integration with the Indian Union, kick-started with the abrogation of Article 370 and Article 35A, it is till today, at best, only a work in progress! Responsibility for its complete integration is cast on every stakeholder, namely, the people of the region, the administrative and revenue officials, the security personnel, the region's political leaders, the Union Government and the rest of Indians. The people of the region have accepted the abrogation of their special status, and eagerly look forward to the transformation of their lives, with uncertainty and anxiety. The officers and security personnel in the newly formed UTs are shouldering a combination of unprecedented responsibilities to contain violence, deliver better standards of life to its people and also truly win their hearts and minds. The region's political leaders, on the other hand, are distraught over losing their statehood to a Union Territory and are struggling for their political survival with incessant claims for restoration of statehood to J&K. The Union Government is reaching out with extended arms generating employment, improving connectivity, wooing development, containing violence and constantly proving its efficacy and transparency.

While all stakeholders, for the first time in independent India, are seriously engaged in integrating J&K with the Indian Union, the real solution to J&K's problems lies in integrating its people with the rest of the Indians, which can only happen with empathizing and re-assuring the hearts and minds of its people. And this is a responsibility that every Indian must now shoulder!

6

KASHMIR: A BATTLE AGAINST KNOWN UNKNOWNS

Abhishek Malhotra

The Union Government of India, in 2019, abrogated the temporary provision of Article 370 and 35A that were the major hindrances in bringing the region back into the mainstream. This structural change has kick-started a transformation process by implementing democratic laws to reverse the damage done in the last seven decades. Over the years, different governments have tried to 'target' militancy, insurgency and extremism through dialogues with separatist leaders. However, these are just the symptoms. The root of the problem is yet to be treated. Once the root is diagnosed, the symptoms will automatically be taken care of.

Until a week ago, my view of Kashmir was broadly based on the print and electronic media which largely talked about the encounters in the Valley, the 'misguided' youth pelting stones and the idea of *jihad* that young minds in the Valley were brainwashed about. Another view of Kashmir was based on the political leaders of the newly formed Union Territory. The political leaders have changed their stance based on the situation in the Valley to support agendas that will help them get back in power.

However, three days in the Valley have changed my perception about Kashmir and the Kashmiri youth. Over those three days, I got an opportunity to interact with the youth in the Valley from different age groups, the brave soldiers deployed by the CRPF and SSB, and Kashmiris serving in the Jammu and Kashmir Police (JKP). One common thing in their stories was that they were all victims in their respective stories and none of them was happy with the prevailing situation. The security forces were in a comparatively better psychological situation since they have been trained for hardships and their passion to serve the motherland keeps them going forward despite the unfriendly residents, difficult living conditions and the three-decade-long insurgency.

The personnel in the JKP have a different view of the entire scenario. JKP is part of all the operations that are undertaken in the region along with the CRPF and the Indian Armed Forces. It forms one of the three layers formed for cordoning off the area of operations. JKP has played a major role in the success of the operations by providing information through locals.

However, there have also been a couple of incidents of JKP personnel helping the militants. This has made them face the heat from both ends (the army and the locals). Any operation in the Valley is bound to draw the anger of the residents against JKP jawans living in that region. The jawans, in the past, have been victims of stone pelting and abusive slurs following the army operations in the Valley. JKP jawans have lost their fellow policemen and their loved ones, and have lost all career aspirations. They are serving the nation hoping that peace will be restored soon. All they ask for is a little respect from their fellow Kashmiris and the armed forces as they too lay down their lives serving the motherland and saving innocent Kashmiris.

The story of the locals is inexplicable. Every story is unique based on their personal experiences and on what they hear from their elders at home and their teachers. On a trek during my visit; I met three young boys under twenty from Srinagar. They had come to visit Pahalgam. Shockingly, they had no hopes of peace and had no education or career aspirations. They just knew what they were hearing from people around them and accepted it as reality. One of them accepted that he goes for stone-pelting because he enjoys the act and it makes him a hero in his peer group. While money is one reason that encourages them to pelt stones, the feeling of being a 'man' pushes them forward. I met another group of men in their mid-twenties who had a different view. They had studied and worked in different parts of the country and had a more open approach. They were forced to come back due to the fear of their families being misled or they themselves being targeted for being Kashmiris.

The boys had mixed experiences as they had made some amazing friends in different parts of the country and also had to face the heat, sometimes, by a selected few for being Kashmiris. According to them, the solution lies in expanding economic opportunities for the youth and providing 'azaadi'; 'azaadi', not from India, but in India.

The experience has changed my fundamental beliefs of what Kashmir is. I believe that the solution lies far away from what a common man perceives. Kashmir is an integral part of India and Kashmiris believe it too. It is not they who need to understand that they belong here but it is for us to believe that they belong to 'Bharat' and hence the new slogan should rather focus on integrating Kashmiris with the mainstream.

The fight for Kashmir is not a physical battle but a psychological war. The solution lies in managing the perception that is created by the so-called human rights activists and local political leaders, who are running the separatist agenda. A similar perception is created by the large media houses, funded by international powers, who want Kashmir to stay isolated for geopolitical reasons to complicate the path of India's growth trajectory. The 9 P.M. debates targeting Kashmiris should shift their focus to the real culprits who brainwash the youth and create a divide. A psychological solution is required for young Kashmiris, so that next time a fifteen-year-old is not misguided towards picking up a stone. The young minds need to be engaged in studies by the formal education system, and provided economic opportunities to engage in work. The unemployment levels in Kashmir are much higher than the national average as they solely depend on government jobs. A young mind sitting unemployed at home, isolated from the rest of the world is bound to believe what he is being told by the people around him.

Kashmir has a tremendous amount of land and resources that need to be utilised by engaging the local youth in work. Empty vessels are bound to make noise. If an average youth is educated and given job opportunities, he is more likely to be engaged in raising a family and occupied with work rather than being misled by the fringe elements of society. Abrogation of Article 370 and the Union Government's attempts to attract private investments in the Valley is one of the initial steps in the right direction. It might not have changed much on the ground in the short run but has made a move in changing the perception towards Kashmir and instiling confidence to people outside Kashmir. It has initiated a structural transformation that will show results in the long run, probably a decade, when a generation will complete education, get engaged in work and be free from the clutches of those spreading hate and keeping them isolated. Once Kashmiris are integrated with mainstream youth, symptoms like militancy, extremism, etc., will disappear permanently.

The article was first published in Rising Kashmir.

7

DEVELOPMENTS IN JAMMU & KASHMIR: A KALEIDOSCOPIC VIEWPOINT

Nidhi Vyas

For the seventh consecutive time, I had the unique opportunity to be a part of the 10th Young Thinkers Meet organised by the India Foundation. This time it was in Jammu and Kashmir. It was an ideal location for the spirit of nationalism. My mixed emotions of curiosity, anxiety and excitement led me to participate with full enthusiasm.

In those three days of the conference, I came to see Jammu and Kashmir under a magnifying glass. Different perspectives of administrator, political leader, security official as well as a perspective of local Kashmiris gave a kaleidoscopic viewpoint for the entire region.

Jammu and Kashmir is undoubtedly blessed with beauty. Due to its history, the people of Jammu and Kashmir have been witness to conflicting situations throughout their generations. The tranquillity created by the landscapes of the Himalayas had seldom affected ordinary life of Kashmiri in a few areas and that is the reason that society there is valiant. They have seen unimaginable situations causing deep emotional, financial and social impacts that are going to last longer than we can think. They are closer to the realities of life and find peace in their faith.

After listening to different viewpoints on Kashmir, I caution that we do not draw inferences for the entire community with just a few stray incidents. They have witnessed circumstances that can shake the very existence of humanity and hence the identity of the Kashmiris cannot be placed in one jacket. It would perhaps be a mistake when quick judgements are made about them without knowing the intent behind it. High dependence on the media and certain sections of people may result in misconceptions.

Amidst all the internal discontent amongst the people of Jammu, POJK, Ladakh and Kashmiri Pandits, the warmth and love they have for the nation is unmatchable. I felt the same spirit of togetherness, even while visiting Dal Lake and Pahalgam. Their smile brings a sense of belongingness for even a first-time visitor.

Undoubtedly, it has extreme potential for development and can compete with other states with zeal after the abrogation of Article 370. Now, the people have placed their hopes on change and development. The pain of history will soon be cured with new changes in the region.

My initial scepticism was resolved after interaction with various stakeholders and it is fair to confess that my perception of the Union Territory of Jammu & Kashmir and its people has changed drastically. Amongst the lush green trees, the grey stories of houses need to be dealt with utmost sensitivity and compassion. Let us embrace their sentiments and sincerely acknowledge them as fellow Bharatiyas, a duty we should abide by as citizens of the nation.

8

"KNOW KASHMIR" BEYOND ARTICLE 370

Sammridh Varma

Article 370 and Jammu and Kashmir—two that continue to matter how intensely discussed—always leave us with new insights and which continue to be important to understand. This was evident at the 10th edition of Young Thinkers Meet (YTM) 2021 organised by India Foundation recently at Pahalgam and Srinagar, Jammu and Kashmir. YTM is an annual get-together organised by the New Delhi based think tank, India Foundation, for individuals (mostly under 35 years) who are driven by the idea of a New India. Here, amidst an immersive discussion with socio-political activists, corporate professionals, journalists, students and scientists from across the country, I gained new and diverse insights into how we can look at Kashmir post Article 370.

While we discussed Jammu and Kashmir, a recurring theme was that there was a need to understand the history and background of Kashmir. The idea of 'Kashmiriyat' is both cultural & political and goes far back to the time of Indian independence. Kashmir has been the hotspot of Buddhism, Shaivism and Sufism which form an integral part of its cultural influences even today. The Gilgit Buddha, Shardha Peeth are the important seat of learning based in Kashmir. Add to that, the philosopher and mystic Abhinavagupta and you get a sense of the stellar cultural identity.

The other aspect of Kashmiriyat is the political identity, which has been in flux since independence but which has its roots in the cultural identity as well. This began with the tussle between India and Pakistan over the state. These factors coupled with the series of assertions for freedom and insurgencies led to J&K being unable to be successfully integrated into the country.

Article 370 may have been initially brought into place in order to protect as well as enhance the cultural and political identity of the people. However, over the years its erosion, many amendments and preferential implementation has led to it doing more harm than good to the state's integration and development. Kashmiris have been marred by the instability, the dynastic controlled governance which has prevented democracy to spread its roots as well as create a general isolation from the rest of India. Now with the abrogation of Article 370, it is time to look beyond. Despite the initial shock and uproar, there is a general understanding in the Valley that Article 370 may not come back and we need to look to build a J&K post this scenario.

At the YTM, I could grasp several key ideas that were presented as the required focus going forward.

Employment, development and people's participation in governance were the three key points raised as requiring focus to fulfil the aspirations of Kashmiris. There is a need to approach the developmental needs of the Jammu region and the Kashmir region differently rather than through one single lens. The suggested themes for development included the need for building connectivity from different parts of J&K to the rest of India. Further, it was highlighted that new urban conglomerates need to be developed. Srinagar and Jammu are currently bursting at their seams and cannot alone signify development for the state. Tourism too needs to go beyond Srinagar Valley and we need to tap into other places of potential. Urgent steps for employment creation remain the key and we need to identify sectors to tap into. The IT sector is one industry that has scope since J&K's cool dust-free climate makes it ideal for the housing of IT servers (Data Centres). Also, the promise to strengthen local bodies of governance in the state must be actualised.

Another suggestion that came up was to concentrate on ending regional disparities in development. This would mean concentrating on Gilgit Baltistan, which is an integral part of India though under illegal occupation of Pakistan at present. Could we not try to undertake voting for the people there, especially those who migrated out of Gilgit Baltistan? Could we not provide a parliamentary seat or reservation in education institutions for the people of Gilgit Baltistan?

There is thus a sense of hope and forward-looking aspirations in the state now. Democracy has now been given an opportunity. In the last two years, there has been much more progress than in the past 70 years. There is more dialogue within the state and with the rest of the country. It is essential now to bring all stakeholders together to push the state's development. The all party meet organised by the Union Government is a great start. The local body elections held was also another step in the right direction. Now what the people of J&K look forward to is their statehood. All steps we take need to be in a direction that leads it closer to statehood.

Change is always difficult, but often when change takes its course, new solutions to problems come up and open new avenues. Let us hope that the present changes in the lives of Kashmiris is for the best and brings opportunities and peace to their lives.

9

KASHMIR, DEVELOPMENT AND DIGNITY: AN ANALYSIS

Dr. Abhishek Pratap Singh

Being a student of diplomacy and international studies, the issue of Jammu and Kashmir has never been evasive from my academic curiosity and research interests, especially when one is an Indian citizen. Quite simply, because it has 'key significance' and relevance for both external and internal factors that relate to India's national interests. This includes relationship with our immediate neighbour, Pakistan, concerns on regional security, renewed terrorism activity and, most importantly, with our constitutional provisions and federal structure of our governance. Moreover, as someone who is passionate about natural beauty, Jammu and Kashmir is like a 'splendid paradise' that has been beautifully described in classic works by several poets and philosophers.

The many years that have been lost due to the militancy in Kashmir, are primarily the outcome of the unrealistic policy choices made by our first prime minister on the subject.

While Sardar Patel, as the first home minister of independent India, dealt with Kashmir (J&K) state in the early years, it was Pandit Nehru who was dealing with this issue later. He openly displayed an approach with a 'soft corner' for Sheikh Abdullah, preferring emotional choices to realistic statesmanship. The geographical location and its strategic significance demanded more prudent and collective decision making on this issue.

Given several other related political developments around the same time, the integration of J&K with India, got unnecessarily complicated with time. A detailed scrutiny of historical documents does suggest that if Patel would have dealt with the Kashmir issue, he would have well acknowledged and understood the peculiar situation of this issue, which Nehru failed to see and act upon.

The understanding of the personality more often influences the assessment of history and political exigencies in any given state. The political developments in Kashmir post independent India also have suffered from this fact. Given the context of Kashmir, it becomes imperative to critically assess and accord whatever due role was played by the then Indian leaders. For reasons of historical balance and holistic interpretation, the understanding must not suffer from any prejudice or misperception.

If, in the changed scenario, the state has made some progress on a certain 'developmental front', then the necessary appreciation and recognition of this needs to be established. Nevertheless, change is something, which is always possible and preferable if it aims at the betterment and empowerment of the common people. States largely direct their public policies to reshape their development priorities and welfare goals. But the problem becomes more challenging when this kind of 'positive change' has to face open contestation from self-serving political groups and their 'unfounded historical narratives' that have been built and cultivated in the minds of people over a period of time to suit their political interests and arrangements.

After spending three days in the Valley in the recently concluded 10th Young Thinkers Meet 2021 organised by India Foundation, a Delhi based well-established think tank, along with other bright and shining minds from different streams and parts of India, we came to know and also realise that Jammu and Kashmir is more than a study and history of contested claims, broken legacies, invented histories and mesmerising heavenly beauty. There are now other valid questions and concerns on genuine people-centric issues like public welfare, housing and health, municipal reforms, infrastructure development, education and training, gender equality, industry and tourism promotion, better trade and commerce, and scope for investment opportunities and employment generation. Perhaps Kashmiri society has taken a 'developmental turn' but the politics of the Valley failed to acknowledge that or played ignorant for vested political reasons.

The first trend that I came across during my visit and also realised in other interactions with locals was the persisting concern and questions about development in Jammu and Kashmir. Having lost much of their time, lives and resources during militancy and political violence, the young Kashmiri, I found is more vocal now with questions and demands for the development in the region. For example,

Abdul (name changed), a tea seller in close vicinity of the old colonial style Iron Bridge in Pahalgam, told me that "You see how dirty it is all around. There is much of tourist inflow with rising footfalls, the city Municipal Corporation needs to be more effective on waste disposal and cleanliness". The efforts to curb 'administrative corruption' in recent years, clamp down on delayed projects and the habit of non-verified public expenditure is no longer a government practice in the Valley.

The new technology based OMMAS (Online, Management, Monitoring and Accounting System) of JK Public Works has improved the pace of work on enhancing rural and urban road connectivity. The newly-launched 'Mission Youth' program will serve as a single window platform for registration under several schemes for Kashmiri youths. The seventeen power projects are likely to be completed next year adding 3,500 MW, making the state power surplus. The BEAM model (Budget, Estimation, Allocation, Management System) of public works has brought about a 'paradigm shift' in the work culture of the Valley. This was reflected in our interactions.

Certainly while acknowledging the benefits to common Kashmiris from the rising tourism, they also want the city to be well maintained and clean, in order to be receptive to outside tourism. The old economic model of Kashmir based on growing saffron; walnuts and almonds was more suited to the Kashmiri elite, while rising tourism and other developments bring an equal and open opportunity for growth to the 'Kashmiri subalterns'.

Secondly, the question of development has to be put

forward within the framework of respect for Kashmiri dignity and culture. The people in the Valley feel proud and are passionate about their rich culture, history, cuisine, language, literature, intellect, music and art, which form the core of what we call Kashmiriyat. In our efforts to build the future of Kashmir, we must always remain considerate to this sentiment and emotions. The call for "Jamhuriyat, Insaniyat with Kashmiriyat", as given by our Late Prime Minister Atal Bihari Vajpayee Ji, is the well-settled and largely accepted philosophy in the Valley. Any governance reform and model of development must keep this idea well established both in its thought and practice.

And thirdly, the perspective on Jammu and Kashmir need not be seen from Delhi-based journalism alone. At the same roadside tea-shop in Pahalgam, another long-bearded local youth came up abruptly to me and asked, "Sir, do you see any change? Do you like the Valley". And then I pushed the discussion pointing to him that of course the place is beautiful, now better secured, people are friendly and welcoming. And then he said, "This is a change, Sir, but it never gets reported by the media as they show us only as a militant-affected place with a fragile security environment surrounded by radical minds". At a time when much of India accepted the perspective from non-resident media groups in the Valley, to me it was more necessary to have a 'prudent approach' based on steady exchange of ideas and openness, while seeking for solutions in Kashmir.

More importantly, we need to avoid any 'detached approach' from extant situations while addressing the concerns of Kashmiris because this will lead to 'radical elements' gaining ground in the Valley.

I am not a man of excellent expertise on Kashmir, but after spending some time in the Valley and after interacting with the youth I can certainly say that the process of development is rolling out there. The administration and the people there both collectively need to be acknowledged and praised for this transformation. Nevertheless, this process of development has to face valid questions on rights and liberty, history and culture, political violence and security, loss of lives in militancy and disenchantment with armed forces and putting right perspectives about the people and the Valley. The complexity of Kashmir history is fertile ground for identity politics. These are all 'sentimental and emotional issues' that occupy and shape the minds of Kashmiri people and need not be put to a 'patriotism test' every second day. What they express is the desire for 'development with dignity'. And with the process of development still unfolding, it is the right time if we also consider and address the issue of dignity of Kashmiris.

To my understanding, the future has to be built on the 'consensual and inclusive model of development' in the Valley and this seems to be the right way ahead, as we look forward to complete integration of Jammu and Kashmir with India. It is now not the time to get lost in the complexity of the past, which suits some sections, but rather look forward to 'progressive solutions' on a range of issues that the people of the Valley are facing.

10

SCRAPPING ARTICLE 370 HAS EVOLVED A VISION AND ENVIRONMENT FOR BETTER HEALTHCARE IN NAYA KASHMIR

Dr. Aakansha Bhawsar

"An ideal society should be mobile, should be full of interesting channels for conveying a change taking place in one part to other parts. In an ideal society there should be many interests consciously communicated and shared. There should be varied and free points of contact with other modes of association. In other words, there must be social endosmosis. This is fraternity, which is only another name for democracy. Democracy is not merely a form of government. It is primarily a mode of associated living, of conjoint, communicated experience. It is essentially an attitude of respect and reverence towards one's fellow men."—**Babasaheb Ambedkar**.

The health and well being of a nation is only as good as the health of its least healthy or the people left behind in the journey of growth and well being. The goal is to reach out to those who are least healthy and those who are left behind by bridging the gaps in the broken systems. The political and social justice systems provide the base to which the systems for improving health and well being are made. As we observe the two years of the Government of India scrapping Article 370 and 35A in the Union Territory (UT) of J&K, we realise that, now more than ever, Babasaheb's idea of an ideal society is being actualised. The universal and fundamental human right of social security and health care to which our brothers and sisters were deprived are now accessible due to mobilisation of national resources because of the abrogation of Article 370. This article shares the idea of holistic human security; it shares the data and observations of well being and peace being secured in the UT of J&K in the past two years of its developmental journey after the abrogation of Article 370. Now more than ever, the communication channels are open, national resources are mobile, national interests are consciously communicated and shared and the collective national sense of belongings is building up, strengthening our Indian democratic fabric.

The last two years have evidently mainstreamed and provided an inclusive and equitable access to national health resources to realise the full potential of health and well being in a dignified manner.

The data speaks and validates the idea, intent and the efficiency of evolving systems and ecosystems in Naya Kashmir. According to the Union Ministry of Health and Family Welfare's report, in the last two years the Union Territory of J&K has achieved a record improvement in the sex ratio at birth from 923 to 976 females per 1,000 males. This record improvement is also achieved in key health indicators like maternal and child health, neonatal mortality rate (NMR) and infant mortality rate (IMR). The NMR came down 22 points from 23.1 to 9.8, IMR reduced 16 points from 32.4 to 16.3 and the under-five mortality rate (U5MR) came down to 19 points from 37.6 to 18.5. The maternal mortality ratio (MMR) decreased and the average number of children per women which is calculated as the Total Fertility Rate (TFR) has improved to 2.0 from 1.4 because of the improved antenatal check-up that has increased from 76.7 per cent to 86.6 per cent and institutional births that have increased. The U5MR has come down because of systems being efficiently implemented for full immunisation of children against preventable diseases and common childhood diseases in the Valley. A comparative study of key health indicators recorded in 2015-16 vs. 2019-20 by the National Family Health Survey (NFHS) also reflects the same positive changes and developments being accomplished in making lives better for the general population in the Valley. The unprecedented 22 points decrease in NMR from 23.1 to 9.8, a 16 point decrease in IMR from 32.4 to 16.3 and 19 point decrease in U5MR from 37.6 to 18.5 speaks volumes and validates the rising and shining idea.

The environment and ecosystem for health and human welfare is evolving with the Government of India (GoI) facilitating several national health related schemes and opening up the environment for private and corporate entities to contribute to the ever-abandoned health challenges like maternal and child healthcare in the Valley. For example, the GoI is now implementing and facilitating national policies and action plans for strengthening health facilities like the Pradhan Mantri Surakshit Matritva Abhiyan (PMSMA), upgradation of neonatal intensive care units (NICUs) and sick newborn care units (SNCUs), and skilled birth attendance (SBA), etc. This accelerated progress and upscaled achievements to make lives better by facilitating necessary interventions in the Valley is possible due to constantly improving the security fabric of J&K. The budgetary allocation of J&K under the National Health Mission for the year 2019-2020 was Rs. 963 crore. Five medical colleges, two All India Institutes of Medical Sciences (AIIMS) and 10 model maternal and child health wings are in the process of being set up. With improving roads, highways, and overall connectivity, the ambulance network to transport critical-care patients, pregnant women especially in rural and difficult to reach medical care is improving. All these systems, ecosystems and environment for healthcare and medical service in our Naya Kashmir is evolving remarkably by democratic facilitation, free movement and exchange of national resources and expertise in the UT. The restrictions and hindrances to social security and healthcare have been abrogated with the scrapping of the constrictive, prohibitive and myopic Article 370. Clearly, the decision has ensured the security, stability, predictability and transparency in the laws required for market access. Due to Article 370 and 35A the investments by the Government of India and private and corporate health institutions to realise the vision of healthcare and welfare of citizens of India was restrictive in J&K. It has opened closed minds and the environment of Kashmir for investments, innovations and incomes. Learning from the past and closing the old obsolete pattern, now J&K is on a new journey for growth and development. Naya Kashmir is evolving and better prepared to deal with public health and humanitarian crises that always used to get sidelined with ongoing conflicts and crises in the Valley.

In conclusion, the UT is observing a positive peace and well being oriented transformative journey. The GoI has ignited a spark of hope, by breaking barriers and investing in the future of the Kashmiri people. I am hopeful that this transformative journey started to include and nurture Kashmir's people and ensure their well being by all means will keep moving.

11

I AM GUPKAR ROAD!

Ujjwal Virendra Deepak and Ashutosh Dubey

I am Gupkar road. I have seen a number of kings, wazirs and sadar-e-riyasats since time immemorial who have ruled over these lands. Right from king Gopaditya of the Brahmin family to the royals of Dogras up to the Muftis and Abdullahs of modern times.

I stretch a kilometre from the United Nations Military Observation Group office to the palace of the last Dogra King, Hari Singh, and have witnessed every churn of events in history. Since independence, I have witnessed a lot of violence and anti-national sloganeering, which has stopped for the last two years. It cannot be claimed that there is complete peace and tranquillity here, but definitely there are concrete steps being taken in the direction of establishing everlasting peace. I am witnessing an increase in the level of affection and affiliation among ordinary Kashmiris with the rest of India which was hitherto missing due to Article 370 and 35A. This land which can easily be compared to

Switzerland was deprived of development and prosperity due to the restrictions imposed by Article 370 and 35A. These articles were implemented due to the extraordinary circumstances under which Kashmir was integrated with India, but their provisions and restrictions proved to be a hindrance in the path of development and prosperity of Kashmir. It restricted people from the rest of the country to purchase land and establish business and industrial organisations which would have provided employment to lakhs of Kashmiri youth. But these provisions brainwashed their minds and lured them into the hands of foreign players.

I take a pause and shivers run down my spine thinking of 19 January 1990 when the loud speakers of mosques started blaring loudly asking Kashmiri Pandits to leave their homeland or face death. Lakhs of Kashmiri Pandits fled for their lives. As per the estimates of the Kashmiri Pandit Sangharsh Samiti (KPSS), 75,343 Kashmiri Pandit families in January 1990 and more than 70,000 Kashmiri Pandit families had to leave their homes and property in the Valley later fearing for their life and safety. They always wanted to go back to their homes but Article 370 and 35A restricted them from going back safely. It is only after the removal of these articles that the Kashmiri Pandits mustered courage to go back to their homeland and many more are planning to do it in the near future. There was a time when most of the Hindi movies were shot in Kashmir. A nation that had just started treading cautiously on the path of economic development viewed Kashmir as a cheaper option of shooting movies than in foreign destinations like Switzerland. Not only did it help in generating employment for thousands of Kashmiri youths, it also helped in installing the feeling of nationalism among them. I was fortunate to watch some of the best movies from the 1960s to 1980s like *Kashmir Ki Kali*, *Silsila* and *Kabhi-Kabhi*, even before they were released. Innumerable movies captured the scenic beauty of Kashmir, but later due to rising tensions the number of movies being made in Kashmir were reduced to single digits. Now the government has announced its new film policy for the re-establishment of the movie industry in Kashmir.

When a Gujarati filmmaker, Vijay Bhatt, makes a movie "*Himalaya Ki God Mein*" casting Manoj Kumar who was born in Abbottabad which is in Pakistan and a Bengali heroine, Mala Sinha, and the entire movie is shot in Kashmir then it not only results in the economic development of the region but also goes a long way in strengthening the spirit of "One Nation". A Gupkar Alliance has been formed by some political parties of Kashmir demanding the restoration of Article 370. I would have never allowed anybody to form such an unholy alliance if I could. My name has originated from Gopadri, an ancient hill and as in the *Mahabharata*, there are Shakunis everywhere, but my countrymen are wise enough to see through their nefarious designs.

Let me take you through two situations. First, a firing between some misguided youths of Kashmir and security forces. As soon as the youths stopped firing, the security forces also did so and tried to convince them to surrender. They surrendered and survived to lead a better life.

Second, a mother provoking her militant son to kill as many security personnel as possible to go to *Jannat*. These contrasting scenes are a challenge for our country and we have to ensure that all the Kashmiri youth feel connected with the rest of India. The existing mindset among some Kashmiri families that the killing of their family members in encounters with security forces, will enhance their social status, needs to be changed. It has to be firmly established in the minds of Kashmiris that anyone working against the interests of India is not a "martyr" but a "terrorist".

Today I am the central avenue of a Union Territory, but I am sure one day I will be the main thoroughfare of a full-fledged state again and will also witness its transformation to a developed and prosperous state of the Union of India. I know it is just a transitional phase when the old order is collapsing and a new order is emerging representing the aspirations of the Kashmiri people. This is a phase of transition from anti-national slogans to chants of Bharat Mata Ki Jai, from guns to guitars, from indefinite curfews to overnight celebrations, from stagnation to development and definitely from the status of a Union Territory to the status of a State of the Union of India.

The chinars will once again swing with their beauty, the Dal Lake will be lively and crowded with tourists and I will still be there rejoicing and witnessing history!

This article was first published in Hindi in the Daily Haribhoomi.

12

CHARTING AN INVESTMENT ROADMAP FOR JAMMU AND KASHMIR

Mishika Nayyar

Jammu and Kashmir stands at an exciting juncture in its economic journey. Often referred to as the 'Switzerland of the East', the region is a treasure trove of natural beauty and rich heritage. Endowed with abundant water resources from three perennial rivers flowing across the region, Jammu and Kashmir also has three agro-climatic zones that have made the region number one in production of saffron, apples, walnuts, and almonds in India. The region has an ideal climate for floriculture and an enormous assortment of flora and fauna including Asia's largest tulip garden.

In order to chart an investment roadmap for this region, it is critical that we understand some basics about the region's economy. The Gross State Domestic Product (GSDP) increased at a CAGR (in INR) of 8.51 per cent between 2015-16 and 2020-21 to reach INR 1.76 trillion (USD 24.28 Bn).[1] As opposed to popular belief that the economy of Kashmir is primarily agrarian, it is interesting to note that agriculture (comprising of crops, livestock, forestry, logging, fishery, aquaculture, horticulture, sericulture, floriculture) contributes only 17.5 per cent towards the (GSDP). This is followed by the contribution of manufacturing, mining, quarrying, construction and utilities towards GSDP at approx. 28 per cent. The lion's share is commanded by the ever-growing services industry like hospitality, tourism, real estate, financial services, transport and communication which contributes 54.5 per cent to GSDP.[2]

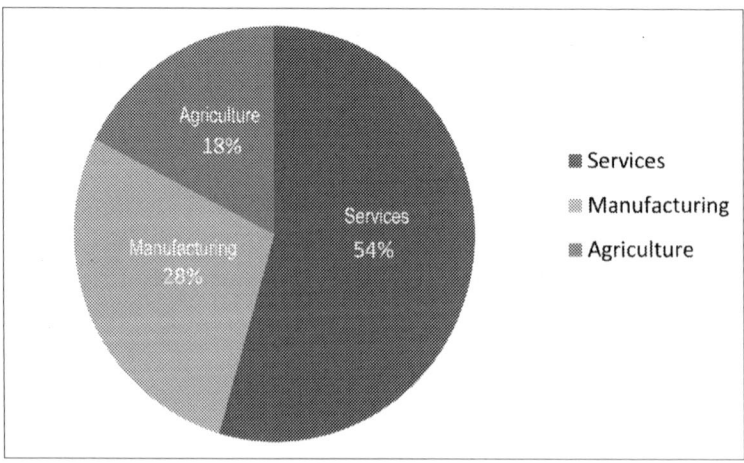

Gross State Domestic Product Bifurcation in Jammu and Kashmir

The vibrant economy of the region is receiving more buoyancy owing to the rising trade. Total exports from Jammu and Kashmir stood at USD 188.18 million in 2019-20. Handicrafts and agriculture products comprise a major share of the exports. During the first three quarters of FY 2019-20, handicrafts worth INR 688.26 crore were exported.

During FY 2019-20 (up to January, 2020), 18.34 lakh MTs of fresh fruit (apples) have been dispatched from the region.[3]

This rising trade coupled with increasing FDI inflows into the region will be critical in taking the economy of this region to new heights. According to the Department for Promotion of Industry and Internal Trade (DPIIT), cumulative FDI inflow in Jammu and Kashmir was valued at USD 0.21 million between October 2019 and December 2020. In less than three months after the revocation of Article 370 from Jammu and Kashmir, around 43 private firms with a proposed investment of INR 13,700 crore have expressed interest to set up businesses in the region. They include Dalmia Cements, Shree Cements, Jakson Group, CVK Group, Paperboat and Design Studios Private Limited having business interests across eight sectors such as manufacturing, defence, infrastructure, technology, information technology, skills and education, renewable energy and hospitality.[4]

The Government of Jammu and Kashmir has already made some headway to enable a conducive environment for investors and this article also aims to chart an investment roadmap for Kashmir which will be "Atmanirbhar" (self-reliant), and sustainable having multimodal connectivity. Having its economy primarily driven by horticulture, handlooms and tourism, the region is set to witness a substantial upsurge in industrial manufacturing with identification of over 6,000 acres for an industrial land bank to develop state-of-the-art infrastructure for industries.

The creation of an industrious economic base in Jammu and Kashmir will not only facilitate trade but also create an efficient logistics ecosystem that will pave the way for welcoming investments. At present, the region has 6,500 large, medium and small industrial operational units. Besides, there are over 20,000 micro industrial units in the formal and informal sector.

To give a major boost to the industry and generate more employment opportunities, DPIIT has notified the "New Central Sector Scheme for industrial development of Jammu and Kashmir" with a financial outlay of INR 28,400 crore in February 2021 and is effective from 01.04.2021 to 31.03.2037. The scheme is applicable for any eligible industrial (manufacturing) entity or eligible service sector enterprise other than those run departmentally by the Government, which is a registered business enterprise under the Goods and Service Tax.[5]

The scheme offers four incentives namely:[6]

1. **Capital Investment Incentive** at the rate of 30 per cent in Zone A and 50 per cent in Zone B on investment made in plant & machinery (in manufacturing) or construction of building and other durable physical assets (in service sector) is available. Units with an investment up to INR 50 crore will be eligible to avail this incentive. Maximum limit of incentive is INR 5 crore and INR 7.5 crore in Zones A and B respectively.

2. **Capital Interest Subvention**: At an annual rate of 6 per cent for a maximum of 7 years on loan amount up to INR 500 crore for investment in plant and machinery (in manufacturing) or construction of building and all other durable physical assets (in service sector).

3. **GST Linked Incentive**: 300 per cent of the eligible value of actual investment made in plant and machinery (in manufacturing) or construction in building and all other durable physical assets (in service sector) for 10 years. The amount of incentive in a financial year will not exceed one-tenth of the total eligible amount of incentive.

4. **Working Capital Interest Incentive**: All existing units at the annual rate of 5 per cent for a maximum of 5 years. Maximum limit of incentive is INR 1 crore.

These incentives are aimed at creating a conducive ecosystem for industry, which attracts investments in focus sectors leading to sustainable, equitable, environment friendly and balanced industrial development thereby creating

employment opportunities for youth, income generation and overall development of the region This scheme also aims to undertake the requisite socio-economic development of the area by identifying the following 14 focus sectors that display the strengths and aspirations of the region.

Each of these sectors has a well-developed, dedicated sectoral policy, which aims to provide for integrated development of various sectors to create a business environment thereby attracting investors to make gainful investments in Jammu and Kashmir and balanced industrial growth at reduced costs leading to creation of employment opportunities, income generation and overall economic development.

For example, to highlight a few, the Jammu and Kashmir Tourism Policy-2020 aims to make Jammu and Kashmir the most preferred all-season tourist destination for domestic and foreign tourists in India by 2025, generate employment opportunities for the people, impart training to around 4,000 tourist service providers over the next 10 years, promote all kind of tourism across the UT, and promote city-wise events and festivals with a pre-defined calendar and promote the same at the national and international levels. This is especially important keeping in mind the increasing footfalls of tourists in the region, which in 2019 stood at 57,920 and 16.16 million for foreign and domestic tourist arrivals, respectively.[7]

The Jammu and Kashmir Captive Power Policy-2020 would encourage investment in establishing captive power plants in the Union Territory (UT). This will not only enable industrialists to cater to the load demand as and when required but will also enable them to sell surplus power in the grid, adding to the total installed capacity through captive generation and further strengthen the process of industrial development. The move would be a step towards bridging the gap between supply and demand and help in the march towards supplying 24x7 quality power to industrialists.[8]

The Jammu and Kashmir Hydro Power and Renewable Energy Policy-2020 would promote the generation of green and clean power using hydro and solar energy, create conditions conducive to the involvement of investors in renewable energy projects, and enhance use of solar energy sources that assist in mitigating environmental pollution.[9]

The Jammu and Kashmir AYUSH Care Investment Policy-2020 aims to realise the obligations of Jammu and Kashmir for providing quality AYUSH care services to citizens within a pluralistic system of integrative AYUSH healthcare, so as to ensure the availability of healthcare at the doorsteps of the common masses. Having more than 300 medicinal plant species and harnessing the distinct positioning of pristine natural resources in the region, it also aims to promote medicinal plants sector in Jammu and Kashmir to conserve, market and process them for establishing herbal industries in Jammu and Kashmir.

For the industry to overall flourish in the region, expanding economic infrastructure and provision of basic services became the need of the hour. This was systematically undertaken in the Prime Minister's Development Package (PMDP) announced in 2015 with an outlay of INR 80,068 crore, which rests on essentially five pillars:

(i) Humanitarian Relief,
(ii) Crisis Management,
(iii) Social Infrastructure,
(iv) Development Projects, and
(v) Economic Infrastructure.

As on March 2021, out of 63 projects pertaining to 15 ministries, 54 projects are being implemented in the Union Territory of Jammu and Kashmir at a cost of INR 58,627crore. These include projects relating to road, power, health, education, tourism, agriculture, and rehabilitation schemes for Kashmiri migrants and skill development sectors.[10]

With a simplified single-window clearance mechanism and right policy ecosystem in place, which is progressive, competitive and investor friendly, Jammu and Kashmir is heading in the right direction as far as its investment journey is concerned. The region not only offers a pristine and pollution-free environment along with one of the lowest industrial power tariff regimes in the country but also a large captive market with easy access to consumers of neighbouring states. With much impetus to build a robust infrastructure and all efforts to connect the region with air, rail and road with the rest of the country, the government is ensuring that the cost of doing business in Jammu and Kashmir remains competitive.

To highlight some initiatives in that direction of creating a robust infrastructure, the Government of Jammu and Kashmir has set up the Jammu & Kashmir Infrastructure Development Finance Corporation (JKIDFC) to raise loans up to INR 8,000 crore for completion of nearly 6,000 projects that were languishing for years. Over 2,367 such projects have been approved with an amount of INR 7125.49 crore and 800 projects worth INR 997.27 crore have already been completed.[11]

Apart from identifying 6,000+ acres for an industrial land bank which is being allotted at concessional rates in industrial areas on lease for 90 years, the Government of Jammu and Kashmir has created a land bank of 29,030 kanals during 2020-21 for setting up of new industrial estates in Jammu and Kashmir. The National Highway Infrastructure Development Corporation (NHIDCL) is developing five tunnels in the UT at a cost of USD 3.42 million. The tunnels will have all-weather access and will be completed by 2024 including the all-weather Zojila Tunnel on NH-1, linking Srinagar and Leh via Dras and Kargil.

An important aspect of attracting investment is the availability of skilled manpower. With a favourable demographic dividend wherein 66 per cent of the population in Jammu and Kashmir is between the working ages of 15 and 59 years, the government is undertaking all measures to ensure the region's rise in the overall Human Development Index.[12] Institutes of national repute ensuring high quality human resources are being established to accelerate overall human development along with creating an industrious pool of workers.

With all cogs in the wheel of investment fitting perfectly, Jammu and Kashmir is set to witness a new dawn of investment and industrial development. The coming up of world class institutes such as IITs and IIMs, two new AIIMSs and seven new medical colleges will bring a new era of development in the region. Pushing the region's overall growth agenda, there is a need for more strategic interventions like how in February 2021, Prime Minister Narendra Modi inaugurated the second Khelo India Winter Games in Gulmarg with the objective of making Jammu and Kashmir a hub for winter sports. Such platforms prove ideal to promote economic development and socio-cultural integration, which is critical to turn the eyes of India towards its important region and also chart an investment roadmap for Jammu and Kashmir bringing in prosperity for all.

ENDNOTES

1. http://mospi.nic.in/GSVA-NSVA
2. IBEF https://www.ibef.org/states/jammu-and-kashmir-presentation
3. https://pib.gov.in/PressReleaseIframePage.aspx?PRID=1601843
4. https://theprint.in/india/43-companies-rs-13700-crore-investment-promise-jk-new-beginning/307398/
5. https://pib.gov.in/PressReleaseIframePage.aspx?PRID=1742402#:~:text=The%20 Department%20for%20Promotion%20of,2037.
6. https://pib.gov.in/PressReleasePage.aspx?PRID=1686743
7. https://www.ibef.org/states/jammu-and-kashmir-presentation
8. https://www.deccanherald.com/national/north-and-central/four-sectoral-policies-approved-to-boost-industrial-growth-in-jk-815824.html
9. https://www.jktpo.in/publications.aspx
10. https://pib.gov.in/PressReleaseIframePage.aspx?PRID=1703792
11. https://pib.gov.in/PressReleaseIframePage.aspx?PRID=1703792
12. https://pib.gov.in/PressReleasePage.aspx?PRID=1730167

13

THE GREY SAFFRON: JOURNEY OF KASHMIR FROM POLITICAL SEPARATISM TO RELIGIOUS SEPARATISM

Swayam Prakash Baral

On 23 July 2021, I visited Kashmir for the first time to take part in a two-day "Young Thinkers Meet", the topic being "Know Kashmir". As an Indian who resides out of Kashmir, I had the opportunity to discuss past and current issues with a few Kashmiri people including bureaucrats and politicians and gained an insight into understanding their perspectives and thoughts about the idea of India and life post the abrogation of Article 370.

Kashmir has been a source of conflict for more than 70 years. In 1947, after Partition, Pakistani armed forces and Pashtun tribesmen attacked the princely state of Jammu and Kashmir. The Maharaja of Kashmir signed a treaty of accession with India, and a dispute started with Pakistan over the region.

In 1948, Pandit Nehru raised the issue in the UN Security Council. A resolution was adopted in the United Nations. Lack of decisive leadership led to the partition of Kashmir for all practical purposes. In my opinion, this decision by Nehru is among his biggest blunders. The debate over the wisdom of this move has continued. It begs the question, Why would Nehru have approached the UN when the Indian army was winning the battle? Had it been given a free hand, the army would have pushed the Pakistani invaders out of the entire territory of Jammu and Kashmir. We would be looking at a very different India today.

Contrary to the requirements of Resolution 47, Pakistan increased its military presence in the area of Kashmir now known as Pakistan-occupied Kashmir (PoK), and 40,000 Hindu families were forced to flee invading Pashtun tribesmen. Pakistan, in all, has initiated three additional conventional wars with India in an attempt to forcefully invade and seize Jammu and Kashmir.

Fast forward to the present day and we know about the numerous terror training camps in Pakistan, the Islamists' *jihad* in Kashmir, and Pakistan-sponsored insurgency which cleansed Kashmir of non-Muslims—300,000 Kashmiri Hindu Pandits were savagely ethnically cleansed from the region. This was over 95 per cent of the indigenous Hindu population. Pakistan still continues to foment violence in the state with cross-border attacks. Radicalisation through mosques, and in more recent times, smartphones and access to the Internet, has opened the floodgates to self-radicalisation.

On 5 August 2021, India marked two years of the

abrogation of Articles 370 and 35A. Article 370 of the Indian constitution gave special status to Jammu and Kashmir. It was another costly blunder by Nehru which stretched the Kashmir issue to unprecedented levels but one that has been rectified by the current government with clear political and social intentions:

- To provide Kashmiris with equal protection under the law and all the rights afforded to an Indian citizen regardless of religion, social class, gender,
- Better access to education and economic development,
- Integration of the people of Jammu, Kashmir and Ladakh with the rest of India,
- Resettlement of the ethnically cleansed Kashmiri Pandits, and
- Equal rights for women.

However, the primary rationale for revoking the special status was to eliminate the terror threat. Home Ministry data shows that terror-related incidents reduced drastically by 59 per cent in 2020 and a further 39 per cent by June 2021 compared to the previous year.

For the last three decades, Kashmiris have been under siege by the proxy war instigated by Pakistan. They had lost their voice and they were kept in abject poverty because of the totalitarian corrupt state government.

The ground reality is that the majority in Kashmir wish to live in peace, and for a better future. At the moment, they are confused as to where this will come from. Pakistan, however, would rather prefer Kashmiri Muslims to die for an Islamic cause and there are elements with this mindset pushing their agenda.

Education, development, improving infrastructure and medical care within the state is key to bringing reformation, and for the 2021-22 financial year, the Central Government has given a staggeringly high budget of Rs. 1.08 lakh crore for the Union Territory of Jammu and Kashmir, the highest ever budget for the state.

The Panchayat Raj system has also been strengthened in the past two years which again is an excellent social improvement enabling people to directly participate in decision making and reducing the burden on the Central Government.

The emerging young leadership in Kashmir acknowledges the mass corruption perpetrated by those few powerful families over the past few decades. It was in their best interests to keep Kashmiris aloof from real development and align them with the narration of a separate nation. The funders and supporters from across the border have been adding to the kitty with their proxy war to keep the state on the boil and prevent peace.

When the rest of India looks at Kashmir, they don't see it as a separate entity. Even though geographical and political integration has taken some shape, a mindset that is distrustful of the Central Government and a bloody religious history, it seems that coexistence is still a long way away for the people of Kashmir to get completely aligned with the idea of India.

14

Experience of Kashmir Hitherto Seen Only on Maps

Chiranjeevi Bhat

Kashmir—when we hear that word, it evokes all kinds of emotions, happiness, sadness, despair and so on. There are many Indians who have never seen Kashmir. And there are some who have seen a map hanging in their schools. Only a few must have really visited Kashmir. As per estimates in 2019, India's population stands at 136 crore. As per UNESCO figures, 8.5 crore tourists visited Karnataka for the first time but Kashmir never gets so many of them. As per Government figures stated in the Rajya Sabha, January 2021 saw a maximum of 2.5 lakh tourists in Kashmir. I am sure not many among them had the opportunity to understand the state, have tea with locals, meet local police, authorities or politicians and learn about the state.

It has been two years since Article 370 was repealed. There definitely was curiosity to know how Kashmir has fared in this period. Many versions were floating around. If the Hindi and English media said one thing, foreign media said different things. This obviously caused some reservations and fear when we undertook this trip to Kashmir. When they came to know I was going to Kashmir, many relatives warned me to be careful and asked if this trip was really necessary. Overcoming all their warnings, I finally landed one Friday in Srinagar. Every step, everything there created some kind of fear all around.

Contrast it with Karnataka—if you find more than a couple of policemen, or if they are hurriedly moving around, the first thought is that some politician may be visiting, or some murder or such crime must have happened. We ask the constable what happened. They don't even reply and get busy with their duties.

However, it is not like that in Kashmir. Every 30-40 metres you will find police or CRPF personnel, at a distance where they can even converse with each other. In any other state of India, policemen posted so close may engage in some conversation, but in Kashmir it is not the situation. They converse among each other very little and interact with the public even less. They are trained and stay alert every moment. Srinagar Airport is located in District Budgam. As you take a cab out of the airport, Jammu Kashmir Police and CRPF personnel take note and watch every single car that passes by. If you have to experience what I am saying, just a look at their faces would be enough—there is suspicion written all over.

When I enquired with the driver, Abdul Mattu, why it is like this, the reply was "Sir, today is Friday prayer time. There is increased security now. It is to prevent stone-pelting and to put fear in the minds of mischief-mongers". For the driver it was commonplace, but for an outsider like me, it was an uncommon and overwhelming experience. It was not just about today, but I had to be careful every day. Recall days when stone-pelting happened. Two stones in hand and two in their pockets were what they attacked the security forces with. This is one grouse the locals have with the security forces. What is odd is that Kashmiris do not hate Jammu Kashmir Police as much as they do the CRPF or the Indian Army. There are some serious reasons for this.

He who served Kashmiri Kehwa, had Sung the Terrorist Anthem

After arriving in Kashmir and in Pampore, a major saffron cultivation centre, how could we return without buying it? I landed in a big shop and was attended by a boy named Abid. Since we didn't know a lot about Kashmir and evinced a lot of interest, he packed some dry fruits for us to consume on the way. He also gave us some food for thought. Even though he hated the Army, he did not make it evident. While straining the Kashmiri *kehwa*, we requested him to sing a song to keep us occupied. He readily agreed and said, "It is not a Bollywood number but one of my own rap compositions". It broke my heart when I realised that he was singing Burhan Wani's song. To summarise, that song was *'Burhan Wani is my Hero, You may have killed him but he continues to live in our hearts. Some day we will definitely fulfil his desire. Kashmir will become independent of India'.* When I took out my mobile and told him that I would record his singing, he said, "No brother, please don't record. The Army may come here right away, shut my shop and take me away. I don't want to end up in that situation".

Do you now know why they hate the Army? The Army, CRPF or J&K Police would never even talk to any Kashmiri without a compelling reason. There are also Kashmiris who offer them kehwa when they see security personnel standing in the sun. If security forces were absent, you can imagine the number of Burhan Wanis that would have emerged here.

India is Good, Will Stay here—Said a Terrorist

The point is simple for us, from Karnataka everything about Kashmir is just like a lesson in a book. But the lesson taught by reality is unforgettable. I have read books written by Walter Lawrence and M.J. Akbar about Kashmir but have totally forgotten about it. However, I will never forget my first-hand experience here. Within two days after I returned to Bengaluru from Kashmir, a gun-wielding terrorist launched an attack at the signal in Kulgam on the Jammu-Srinagar Highway. This is the reason why, people say, the situation in Kashmir is so unpredictable; we can never predict what will happen when. It was like any other traffic signal in Bengaluru when I visited the same spot. This terrorist attack can give you an idea as to how things change drastically in a matter of time.

We learnt later that, on that particular day a Pakistani terrorist was killed in an encounter after a chase in his hideout in a building by the CRPF. An AK56, an RPG grenade and other ammunition were recovered from him. I asked the IPS officer who was part of the team whether, he knew what the terrorist's objective was. Was he planning something big?

The reply was shocking, "No, he came prepared to die". If he was not prepared to lay down his life, why would he open fire at policemen or the CRPF? He continued, "No, this is what normal people think. If we say the same thing, people will laugh at us. We have the right evidence." This triggered my curiosity, "How do you conclude that he came on a suicide mission?" The answer was, "When we sent his body for post-mortem examination, we found that his genital areas were clean shaven, body was perfumed and on top of it, he also carried an extra bottle of perfume." If you are wondering what is the relation between him being on a suicide mission and his shaving his private parts and wearing perfume, you are not alone. Even I wondered what that meant and the basis of the officer's conclusion. He continued, "They believe that if they die a martyr, they will go to *Jannat* and there would be 72 virgins waiting as a gift for him. That is why they shave clean, take a shower and wear perfume, so that everything is easy and he is ready for the treatment in *Jannat*. This is the normal practice of all suicide bombers."

These are the things you learn first-hand when you are in Kashmir. Pakistani terrorists who arrive in India want to die within a couple days for another reason. They arrive from Pakistan with the help of their handlers in India and remain hidden somewhere. On the pre-determined day, they go to carry out their suicide missions and give up their lives.

When they indoctrinate terrorists in Pakistan, they keep brainwashing them saying Islam is in danger in India.

Muslims are killed every day and are in difficulty. A person who is conditioned to think like this, realises on his arrival in India that Muslims lead normal lives and is impressed. The handlers worry that seeing the happy condition of Indian Muslims, the 'terrorist might change his mind and hence, plan the mission within days of arrival.

A terrorist apprehended by the Jammu Kashmir Police was asked if he thought Muslims in India live a miserable life or if Islam is in trouble! Even before the police personnel could complete their question, the terrorist replied, "No Sir, India is good. We haven't seen any Muslim or Islam being in any kind of trouble. On the contrary, all of them seem to be very happy. The scenes that were projected on the screen in my camp were of total bloodshed. But I see that Muslims go to homes of Hindus, to shops of Hindus and vice versa too. Sir. I want to remain in India, please" recalled an investigation officer.

Even in Kashmir, Muslims wearing burqas or skull caps is not very common. Their usual attire is normal kurta and pyjama for men and women wear Kashmiri dress similar to chudidars. I checked with the driver if it is not *haram* to be that way. He replied, "Look Sir, we are worried about our food. It makes no difference to us what we wear. We fight in the name of Shias and Sunnis and it is not worth it. We don't wear skullcaps or burqas. I am not even able to offer my *namaz* many times. If it is *haram*, Kashmir would have been filled with *haraamis*. Sir, we have reached the airport. Have a nice journey. Please call me without fail, the next time you are in Kashmir." He bid me a fond goodbye. The driver also sent me a friend request on Facebook and even likes the photos of our God that I post on Facebook. He wished me for Varamahalakshmi vrata festival and jokingly asked me to send *prasada* on Ganesh Chaturthi.

This is real Kashmir. It is not only the violence portrayed by various media. Kashmir is a beautiful place. It also has some risks, but you can enjoy the place with some care.

15

FROM IDEOLOGICAL SAFFRON TO KASHMIRI SAFFRON

Aparajita Tripathi

"*Mijaaz nahin milta mera*", the spectacled JK Police force officer muttered, as he sat down on the lush green grass surrounded by tall pine trees with the Pir Panjal range silhouetted against the type of sky that gave it its blue.

It was his response to my question on whether he enjoys his profession that compels him to keep Wandering, searching for all that is dark, dangerous and dysfunctional. Aspiring to become a nuclear geologist, a career focus I had never heard from anyone in all the time I have walked on this Earth, he had traded his interests and his '*mijaaz*' (the beautiful Urdu word for the relatively undeserving 'temperament') for the only service employment that offers a guaranteed income in the ravaged climes of Kashmir. He said that the policing profession requires a temperament much distanced from the delicate, studious tendencies that he originally had, and would have continued had family pressures not forced him to join the ranks.

While sharing his thoughts with two of us, he was simultaneously breaking into the alertness of a police officer watching his friends at a distance, stare at him; and breaking away from us to stare into the idyllic silence that just about any spot in Kashmir offers. At that point, he could be talking to himself or to us; it wouldn't have made a difference. People are often the most comfortable expressing heartfelt confessions to strangers who offer a promise of anonymity, irrelevance, and unrepeatability.

I gazed into his eyes, and wondered about the dreams of a young boy who wanted to pursue the core of geological physics but ended up becoming a pursuer of rebel human beings. At that point, the story of Mahroof*,13, (name changed to protect identity) and countless stories of similar-aged young boys and girls, outside Kashmir, became one in their disappointments of transitioning into adulthood.

As I write this on the 75th anniversary of Indian Independence, and 75 years of the Kashmir conflict, it is these stories that make me question: In the differences between Kashmiris and the rest of the country, did we forget how similar we are?

The Journey into Kashmir: Young Thinkers' Meet

Some weeks ago, I was fortunate enough to attend the Young Thinkers' Meet held in Srinagar and Pahalgam, on the fascinating topic of Article 370. The journey; spread over three days, two flights, and 100 km of inland Kashmir bus travel; resulted in thousands of seconds of deliberation and continuing poignant moments of introspection that see no end in sight.

The sight that immediately arrests one's attention in Kashmir is the continual arrays of camouflaged soldiers standing on both sides of the road (I now learn they are called Road-Operating-Party (ROPs) across the entire city of Srinagar and its outskirts. The sense of chaotic normalcy seen in almost all parts of India, is miraculously absent in Kashmir, for a burgeoning chaos in Kashmir is often a sign of impending danger. In UP and Bihar, almost all non-descript lane corners are crowded with *paan* shops and *thela* joints but similar locales in Kashmir have military bunkers or CRPF units or army vans. It's also one of the few places where the police, military and paramilitary forces work in close coordination on an everyday basis.

Surprisingly, Srinagar is hardly the place that evokes the romanticism of Kashmir's beauty. For a good few hours, we were struck by how hot it was, contrary to our expectations. It was only after some time, when we were somewhere on the outskirts of Srinagar, headed for Pahalgam, flanked by paramilitary patrol units on both sides offering us the privilege of security in the strife-laden place; that we realised the grandeur of Kashmir in all its glory.

Honestly, Kashmir is beautiful. It has been blessed with a stunning exquisiteness not known in other places, even in other hilly regions. I muttered somewhere along the bus journey, "It's worth fighting for". As we passed along the road, we saw a concentration of shops laden with wooden logs and wooden shafts, only to realise it's a cricket bat manufacturing cluster—the site of the famous "Kashmir willow". As a fellow passenger exclaimed, "Does India really play with so many bats"? We were struck by the copious manufacturing of bats in a region we would not normally associate with the Indian cricket team.

That's the irony of being in Kashmir. It's central to every Indian's heart, one of our long-standing issues in the subcontinent, and pivot of every political discussion, and yet, we hardly speak of it as a geographical entity disconnected from strife, in terms of its richness, its industry, its aspirations or its unique everyday problems.

That topic came up time and again when we finally got to interact with Kashmiri leaders in the picturesque resort in Pahalgam, during the inaugural session of the conference. Characteristically, I chose a seat at the last table, happily situated next to a window.

As the words started flowing, I couldn't help notice the absolute remarkability of the moment. Dyed in shades of saffron, we couldn't be more on the opposite side of every Kashmiri leader's point of view, and yet here we were happily ensconced in a room trying to understand each other. The leaders on this side of the debate waxed eloquent about the Indic roots of Kashmir—the land of syncretism of Hindu and Buddhist thought, with ancient historical accounts of how Ashoka founded Shrinagari (outskirts of modern Srinagar), how Shankaracharya opened the southern door of Sarvajñapîmtha (Shardapeeth) by defeating all scholars and attaining transcendent wisdom (His temple, maintained by 9 Rifles, is still an important historical site), how Abhinavgupta completed Tantraloka (encyclopaedic form of Kashmir Shaivism aspects) and how a conversation between

Vasishta and Rama is an integral part of the *Moksopaya Shastra*, written on top of Praduymna hill in Srinagar.

Parts of this we know through common knowledge, and the other part of how Kashmir gained two-edged independence is also known to a majority of us—that Maharaja Hari Singh initially didn't sign any instrument of accession to either Pakistan or India, fearing that the Muslim majority of Kashmir wouldn't want to side with India, and the Kashmiri Hindus and Sikhs would have a hard time in Pakistan. Pakistan was not content with this stance and sent in forces to wrest power forcibly, if necessary. The Maharaja appealed to the Indian Government for military help, which could only be given if Kashmir signed the Instrument of Accession. Kashmir was rescued once the Instrument was signed, albeit with a conditional proviso of a possible plebiscite later once the dust had settled. The rest is history.

Unfortunately, wikipedia sweeps all of this history with an anti-Hindu brush, in a major ideological departure from its early days of neutrality. Sources quoted for references are works by British historians, many of whom had a traditional penchant for being agent provocateurs, inciting fire where there was none; and by Islamic scholars with a decided point of view on the 'atrocities against Kashmiris'. Indians have their own version of verbal history—content with their *smriti* and *shruti* techniques, they haven't till date mastered the art of winning the war of narratives with the written word.

The Provocation of Ideas

All of these points came up time and again by agents of both sides of the divide. However, it was the Kashmiri leaders' point of view that was new to us. Person after person reminded us, correctly, that Kashmir was not rescued from Pakistan in 1947 by the Indian Army alone; that it happened primarily due to the Kashmiri Muslims who fought alongside the army, as they were the first line of defence. Many of those fighting the insurgents were also members of the then National Conference. They reminded us that while the nation comes down heavily against Kashmiri Muslims, it forgets that, as a line oft-quoted says, *"2,500 Kashmiri Muslims lying in the graveyards of Kashmir have a Pakistani or a militant bullet in them"*.

The leaders reminded us that the media peddles a narrative that the rest of us Indians love to lap up of the Kashmiri Muslim at war against the Indian state, the stone-pelting, the border-crossings, the sleeper-cells, the young educated lads brandishing guns. Yet, while we hate a Burhan Wani, why do we forget that the young JKF policemen, like the police officer (above) whose temperament is dissociated from the rigours of policing, fighting against the enemy, have also grown from Kashmiri soil.

In a closed-room setup, they admitted that bringing back Article 370 is next to impossible even by the same people who took it away. However, they were jointly crestfallen at the snatching away of statehood. *"It is humiliating to be stripped of powers"*. Another one said that like all of us coming from states around the country, they too wish to devise their strategy and vision for Kashmiri development. *"We wish to tell the world that J&K produces doctors and engineers, while Azad Kashmir (PoK) exports labourers"*.

It was clear that there was an escalation of the fringes by the media, which has the same template for almost all stories in the rest of India too. The leaders brought focus to the paradoxical Kashmiri identity typified by hesitation, suspicion, a sense of urgency and a tendency to be misunderstood.

They said that it was the moderate Kashmiri Muslim who had accepted the unthinkable—a BJP government in the state, *'putting their faith in the hands of a party not only seen as a Hindu party, but one that had removed Article 370 in its manifesto'*.

The appeal hit hard. I had tears trickling down my cheeks. Briefly disturbed, enamoured by the appeals of the articulate  Kashmiri leaders (much in contrast with several of the bumbling regressive leaders in the rest of the country), I started wondering if we were wrong somewhere in our assessment of the land with a million stories, and used my position at the back to gaze out of the window.

Against the stunning scenic view, amidst chinar trees with a Christmas-tree like canopy, and the sloshing sounds of sea-green crystal-clear waters, I saw dozens of camouflaged soldiers walking in file, perambulating the resort's boundary to keep guard. A few metres from the room, seated amidst an assemblage of trees in a cosy spot, were some other leaders enjoying a hearty lunch. It was the chasm between the two sets of people that brought me out of my emotional disturbance. As the conference discussions intensified, my eyes kept darting to things happening outside the window, with *'Hukus Bukus'* playing in the inside of my head as an earworm.

The tea break gave us much-needed relief. After all, who wants to be holed up in a room when you have the most picturesque evening in Kashmir to gaze at. Over authentic kehwa with shreds of almond, we engaged in an informal chat with leaders who now, outside the purview of a staged-led atmosphere, were clearer in their points of view. To a pointed question that I posed regarding the role of the elder Kashmiri community in nurturing or hushing the voice of rebellion among young native boys and girls, I was handed back a comment that has stayed with me since, 'Are you going to punish people for thinking the way their context has shaped them?' *Had you been born as a Muslim in Pakistan, would you have still thought the way you think now?"*

Detailed discourse is a double-edged sword. It opens your mind to ideas you wouldn't have entertained earlier, but at the same time, leaves you conflicted and solution-less. If the entire world went about understanding everyone else's context and assumptions, mankind would not get any work done.

The truth is, the world runs on an exactly opposite idea. More things in existence owe their genesis to someone's whim than to carefully thought out constructs, as much as we would like it to be. Thanks to Radcliffe's whimsical approach to the division of a region from the inside of a room within seven days, it is clearly a mirror for us on both sides of the Indo-Pak border.

The idea stayed with me. In the course of the day, we met two young IPS officers who hail from and work in Kashmir. Their story was quite stunning. They remember their childhood as an Elysian dream, playing in orchards, climbing up hillocks, and throwing apples at each other—something distant from what we would have imagined hearing. Now their work exposes them to the vagaries of Kashmir, the dark side unknown to their childhood alter egos. During the ensuing discussion, it became clearer that unlike the earlier Nineties, technology has allowed an infusion of knowledge and opportunities to the endemic Kashmir Valley population who now carry international aspirations; it has also proven to be an effective tool in the hands of the Other in the dissemination of dangerous ideas. Restricting access to prevent brainwashing also means restricting development and awareness. It's a problem without a clear solution.

While we kept listening to speaker after speaker, my eyes gazing firmly outside the window were observing the goings-on in the green landscape. Many of these leaders who had moved us to tears were now huddled over a grand table laden with Kashmiri delicacies, sometimes guffawing, sometimes giving bytes to journalists. I could not help thinking that some of these fair, rosy-red cheeked, tall, articulate, well-mannered people have been anti-India at some point or the other. That they have come to have a discourse with a set of people on the absolute opposite side of the divide, was a testament of victory for India Foundation

From Ideological Saffron to Kashmiri Saffron   87

in particular, and for Indian outreach to them over 75 years, in general.

As the evening afforded us a kehwa break, I ventured to the far side where sitting comfortably under a giant tree that overlooked the entire picturesque road and the green-blue waters, were two young camouflaged officers, who I later came to know were from the Shastra Seema Bal. I asked them if they liked it here better. One of them, looking away, simply replied, *"Garmi kam lagti hai, par wahan kuch naxal hote they, yahan to sab naxal hain'* (It's less hot here. But, in those areas, a few would be Naxalites (used loosely), but here in Kashmir, everyone is a Naxal (anti-establishment).

I then took a picture with them, a picture that's possible only in conflict zones—I, in a deep red fine *kota doria* salwar kameez, with two soldiers in camouflage hiding their weapons out of camera view, against a scenic backdrop more suitable for movies and romantic getaways, than for conflicted terrorist operations.

We rounded off the evening with a stirring fireside chat with Ram Madhav ji and top leaders from the RSS and from Kashmir. Quite a motley mix that was. Here, it was time for the participants to speak, share and ask, and the words continued late in the night.

Pir Panjal and Men in Uniform

Early next morning, we started scaling up a mountainous road to undertake a short trek. For most of us on the wrong side of the healthy quotient, the trek proved arduous, only to realise disappointingly that our final destination was actually the base camp for serious trekkers aiming to scale the Pir Panjal trek.

Asthmatic yet energetic, I still scampered up like a mountain goat, wanting to be the first one to reach the top; but the last 50 metres felt difficult with me, coughing and breathing like a bronchial patient, and at some point felt like giving up, until a camouflaged officer held my hand supporting me all the way up to the base. The one with glasses, introduced in the beginning of this essay, was shining blistering red with the heat and the weight of a gun and bullet proof vest, and the climb; yet, he took on the additional effort of helping a struggling girl.

Standing in the middle of verdant green grass, surrounded by the Pir Panjal range, the largest mountain group of the lesser Himalayas, dotted with tall oak trees, and a group of Kashmiri shepherd children frolicking with an adorable lamb; it felt like it was straight from the movies. If only a camcorder could take a 360-degree view, we would feel *'ye haseen vaadiyan, ye khula aasman'* was being crooned in the background. And in the middle of this picture perfect setting, we found ourselves face to face with a dignified officer from the J&K Counter Terrorism force whose repertoire is full of stories of men, some of whom had gone to 'the other side', and some who came back disillusioned, and are now involved in regular farming.

I was quite nonplussed by the regular sprinklings of stories of men who 'go over to the other side', come back and are now part of the Kashmiri citizenry, all in the knowledge of the law keepers like this person who not only went out, came back, but realised that solutions to his problems lay in this country, and therefore followed it up with electoral victories. It's a typification of a geography that is so different from all the states we come from where such a categorisation would be a Sentence For Life for the entire family.

On our way back trailing down the mountains, I spoke to an animated officer of the JK Police, while reflecting internally that with his natural dramatic relish, he should have been in the theatre. Tall, well-built, possibly on the other side of 40, bright gray eyes, unlike the silent forces that walked next to us; he was garrulous with spicy anecdotes, and entertaining. Hailing from Udhampur, he was proud of his son who, he said, could become a great officer, although he wanted him to become a sportsperson. He told me that Udhampur is now almost free of militancy and, again with a dramatic flourish, said forcefully, *"If you left this gun anywhere in Udhampur, by evening, someone would clean it and return it to you"*. He added, *"If you don't believe me, ask this fauji"*. The 'fauji' was from the SSB, walking absolutely quietly in front of us. He hailed from one of the central states. This man knew that somewhere people like us would tend to believe the armed forces more than the word of the J&K police. I laughed much red and embarrassed, even though I was credulously lapping up everything he said and enquired if the gun was heavy. He suddenly thrust it into my hands, and said, 'Find out for yourself.' And boy, was it heavy! It took me some steps to regain my composure after handling an approx. 4-kg gun, let alone the weight of realisation of what I was holding. In my mind, where thoughts were progressing at the speed of zillions per second, flashes of young Kashmiri boys arming themselves regularly kept occurring to me. Kashmir imports guns and makes bats; but learns to play with the former in its adolescence.

In no time, we were making our way to the hotel to go on with our journey to the hotbed of Kashmiri politics, back to Srinagar. On the way, we met several men who offered to sell us standard Kashmiri fare—pashmina, salwar kameez, pistachios, walnuts, saffron—but would not come close upon seeing military men around us. Imagine! Living your life constantly in fear of the eyes of guns and authority-wielding men on you.

Governance and Departure

Srinagar is not beautiful like the rest of Kashmir, albeit more than the rest of India. Leaving the cool climes of Pahalgam far behind, we went straight to Centaur Hotel, famous as the residence-for-house-arrest of Kashmiri politicians during the abrogation of Article 370. Interactions started with Apni Party President, Altaf Bukhari, who too, mourned the loss of statehood, of the lack of tributes for hundreds of Kashmiri Muslims who had laid down their lives against terrorism, for not being understood among Indians.

By now, we could see how they see us, and how they see themselves through our lens—misunderstood and unappreciated. Amongst this chasm of understanding, India-sympathising Kashmiris feel lost. In their assessment, they are neither here nor there. By chance of their circumstances, they cannot see India the way the rest of us do, but their approximate loyalty is still questioned. And the terrorists hate them, for these people, by virtue of their work on the ground, tend to lighten the make-believe hatred that the terrorists wish to create. No wonder, in about two weeks after we left the Valley, Apni Party's leader Ghulam Ali Lone, was gunned down by terrorists.

We had heard the people, the CRPF, the leaders on both sides, and now we were face to face with the people tasked with the responsibility of ushering in Kashmiri development—Lt Governor and Chief Secretary—who hail from UP and Bihar. As they rattled out developmental metrics, I forgot for a few moments the site of our audience; it felt like we were back in a governmental programme in New Delhi. The temporary departure into the ordinary was quite relieving.

Various developmental activities are being undertaken under the Prime Minister's Development Package, but there is significant focus on reforming the bureaucracy which, thanks to years of Pampering, had grown apathetic, unmoving, and inertia-ridden, as also testified by some members of Jammu and Ladakh we met along the way. It will be a long time before one can conclusively say if the pace of change has been instrumental in bringing about a change in the hearts of its people too, who otherwise are so wrapped up in their hatred against this nation that protects them.

We couldn't see Srinagar in its full finery as the day was chosen to be suitable for a Presidential Visit, which means routine stops and diversions in the rest of India, but complete curfew in Srinagar. We had the good fortune of finishing an activity without which one's trip to Kashmir is not considered complete—leisurely in a houseboat floating serenely on the Dal Lake. From the top of the houseboat, one saw such golden hues of the setting sun that any description would only lack words to bring out the splendour of such a scene. Every angle was like a Renaissance painting. Kashmir is so magnificently beautiful that it rubs off some of its sheen onto those within its arms. There could be no other reason but this, that at least four times in Kashmir, I was asked/spoken to in Kashmiri, assuming I hailed from there. With a standard wheatish brown skin, I cannot pass muster as a Kashmiri on any other day, but for the resplendence of the atmosphere.

Soon, after a night-halt in a luxurious hotel with wooden interiors, where we exchanged thoughts; we climbed 250 stairs in a stopover at daybreak in Shankaracharya's Shiva temple on the Shankaracharya hill on the Zabarwan range, 1,000 feet from the Valley. Fortunately, it was the first Monday of the month of Sawan (*as per the Indian calendar it is considered extremely holy for worshipping Lord Shiva*).

Post that, we headed back to our humdrum, mundane lives. Wanting to pick up some clothes as gifts for our parents, I asked our driver on the way to the airport to take a detour. This last bit was quite expository in the Kashmiri way of everyday life, which we as tourists seldom experience. Given that the entire city was barricaded during curfew, our driver was stopped multiple times for questioning. He said angrily, '*Aap hain to chhod de rahe hain, akele hota to batate*'. (Because you are sitting, they are leaving me, else would have given it badly to me).

He was the first Kashmiri among all I had spoken, whose hatred was not cloaked in the presence of tourists. At 23, it's difficult to hide emotions. I asked him the reason for his *talkhi* (bitterness in Urdu). He answered our questions as directly as possible, *'No, none of us want to be with Pakistan, but we don't want to be with India either. Azaadi is what we want'*. The more he ranted and raved, the more intense the discussion became, where my words were also starting to become tinged with anger given the levels of gas-lighting that I could see was on display. It's not his fault. The result of years of selective storytelling through multi-layered communication channels, this indoctrinated one-sided worldview is not going to alter overnight in favour of any policymaking, let alone that which comes piggybacking in saffron clothes. I asked him if he hated the army or the police more, his answer was direct. *'Army buri hai, police aur bhi badtar'*. (*Police is worse than Army*). The police bear the brunt of their ire, since many of them hail from the same villages unlike those in the army who come from outside. The Army comes in with more strategic operations, but with deeper penetration; the police get involved in all kinds of problems and thus earn more ill-repute.

The Kashmir separatist movement has traversed the path from being a political quagmire to one pivoted on religious separation. Almost as a list mugged up for exams, this 23-year old could rattle off all the so-called 'injustice(s)' against Muslims in one go—Gujarat, Babri Masjid, Bombay riots, Muzaffarnagar, etc. But he became silent the moment we talked about the Kashmiri Pandits.

That's the dangerous problem. It's no longer a geographical or political crossfire in favour or against Pakistan. It's now taken on the green mantle of being in favour of Islam. The Kashmir separatist movement has traversed the path from being a political quagmire to one pivoted on religious separation.

All this was with a touch of dramatic irony. His self-affected voice of complaint was listing out the wrongs of the Indian State set to the tune of his playlist that carried an air of sadness through the unmistakable voice of Lata Mangeshkar – *'Yun hasraton ke daag'*, and *'Waqt ne kiya haseen sitam'*. Fascinated, I enquired as to why he listens to such old songs unheard in any young one's playlist today. He said reflecting, 'All of us are marred by pain, and it's only painful songs that appeal to us.' His favourite singer was Lata Mangeshkar. Somehow that brought me incredible satisfaction, that despite all the bitterness we are conjoined at birth and have some threads of culture that are sewn into our being.

It's true that almost anyone you speak to sounds like they were painted with pain. Some more, some less, but the pain can be seen—as unmistakably clear as the pebbles under the crystal blue waters of the Tso Moriri lake. This young driver complained that all that they have seen since childhood is a *'zulm ka daur'* (reign of injustice); the really old man who was turned away at a crossing by the police had a bent back and closed fists, reflective of one who has seen great misery; the aged salesman who sold me dozens of suits and thought I was a Kashmiri said in reply to my plea for a discount, *'I don't have money or authority. I have a huge house, my children are settled and we two live alone. You take my keys, I have an old car, take it and enjoy the city. We have homes but no life. Come and live at no cost, we will be happy to host you.'* He too said in a manner of men whose pain has become so ingrained that it no longer evokes emotion.

The poor in the rest of India are very different from the Kashmiri poor. Everyone has a home, decent clothes on their backs and enough to eat. What they don't have is livelihoods. Despite the hard-wrenching laments, interestingly, what no Kashmiri talks about is the benevolence of the Indian State towards Kashmir. It is not what you would call poor, a fact understood by those coming from the rest of India. We have all seen poverty in our native lands. Uttar Pradesh, my home state, has millions of people in shabby tenements in villages, with little to eat, and nowhere to live. Cities are full of people living on streets with less than one complete meal a day. Villages and decrepit colonies have people fighting for space and for resources. But, the poor in other states are very different from the Kashmiri poor. It's a state where everyone has at least one house, a small orchard with walnut trees that can give up to Rs. 50,000 a year.

Everyone, like this salesman, has a big home, decent clothes on their backs and enough to eat. What they don't have is livelihoods or freedom. When I had asked the bespectacled JK Police officer who wanted to study nuclear geology, if there was scope for it in his state, he had replied, *'One doesn't need it. In Kashmir, one can stay all our life without working and still have enough to get by.'* If only people were that generous with self-assessment, as they are with the assessment of others, the world would have been a different place. I had the feeling that it's a false notion that Kashmiris don't want us to come. They really want us to visit, for tourism is their main source of earning, but they definitely don't want us to stay.

The return flight was quiet. My mind was not. I had gone

to Kashmir with a one-dimensional saffron view, but I came back conflicted. Not in the genuineness of our case, but in the experiential practicality of theirs. In the dashed hopes of the youth, in the cry for freedom, in the feeling of 'caged' atmosphere, in the feeling of being untrustworthy, in the lack of options for the people of the state.

Policymaking continues over the years. But lives are finite. Many of them were born with a feeling of being golden birds in cages, and will die with that, without experiencing the complete set of joys that is available to people in the rest of the country. Some of the blame lies squarely on their shoulders, some to their indoctrinated upbringing, but a large part on the vagaries of circumstances of birth—almost for like the rest of us.

While we continue to hope that some day the Kashmiris will see the goodness within us, the commitment to the cause of their development, and the lack of ill-intention among all Indians, I believe we may want to perceive them a little less jingoistically, and a little more humanely, to accommodate and open lines of conversation. This is in our self-interest, as a tribute to the countless soldiers who have been the *purnahuti* in this *yagna* of possession.

The good thing is that the tiredness with eternal conflict and the abrogation of Article 370, has dimmed the fire of rebellion. The entire appeal was for a return to statehood, which is a progressive step, should you view it in the entirety of the conflict. As the story of Samudra Manthan (Churning of the Ocean) from the *Bhagavata Gita* goes, along with the nectar of immortality, came the lethal poison, Halalhal. Shiva then had to contain it in his throat to save us all, but we are in kalyug, and here in the absence of earth-bound gods, we must all partake a bit of it.

All of us dyed in various shades of saffron, came back with a wider palette of underlying greys. It's ironic that the anathema of Kashmir to all thoughts of saffron, is offset by their closeness to the real saffron—the source of their income, their export, and their USP.

16

Report Tenth Young Thinkers Meet

PAHALGAM AND SRINAGAR
JULY 23-25, 2021

INAUGURAL SESSION:
SHRI SHAURYA DOVAL

The inaugural session of India Foundation's tenth Young Thinkers Meet, held in Kashmir from July 23 to 25, 2021, was chaired by Shri Shaurya Doval, Member, Board of

Governors, India Foundation. Shri Doval described that holding of the tenth edition of the Young Thinkers' Meet in Kashmir was an important chapter in the journey of India Foundation. He said that the larger purpose of the Meet was for the delegates to brainstorm and come up with ways to assimilate and integrate the people of the Union Territory of Jammu & Kashmir with the larger Indian polity. He advised the delegates to come up with solutions to the larger question of what we, as Indians, could do to convince the world that Jammu & Kashmir is a rightful part of India. With these brief remarks, Shri Doval opened the Meet.

Keynote Presentation: Shri Alok Bansal

Shri Alok Bansal, the Director of India Foundation, addressed the delegates on 23 July 2021. He gave the day's keynote presentation on 'Jammu & Kashmir—Past, Present & Future'. The session was moderated by Shri Aaditya Tiwari. Shri Bansal established that Kashmir was a part of India by citing evidence across historical scriptures such as the *Rajatarangini*. However, the narrative that Kashmir was not a part of India was conceptualised and perpetuated largely under British colonial rule.

He then moved onto the history of contemporary Kashmir and highlighted the fact that the Instrument of Accession signed by the then ruler of Kashmir, Maharaja Hari Singh, was not any different from the instruments signed by contemporary rulers of other princely states. However, certain provisions of the Instrument which led to the formulation of Article 370 and Article 35A were inimical to the development of the then state of Jammu & Kashmir. The abolition of these provisions in 2019 has opened new doors for Jammu & Kashmir and has led to an emergence of grassroots democracy in the Union Territory.

Contemplating about Jammu & Kashmir's future, Shri Bansal asserted that the way forward for the Union Territory of Jammu & Kashmir would start with a successful completion of the exercise of delimitation that would not only address the demographic imbalance inherent in the political representation across the areas of the Union Territory but also provide rightful representation to representatives of Pakistan Occupied Jammu & Kashmir (POJK). The people of India need to make an attempt to include the political aspirations of people across the border in the occupied territories. Moving on to the topic of economic development in Jammu & Kashmir, Shri Bansal said that for Jammu & Kashmir's economic development, investment from the private sector is crucial and that the dependence on government schemes would not be enough.

Plenary Session I: Shri Sajad Lone

The first plenary session at India Foundation's tenth Young Thinkers Meet, held in Kashmir from July 23 to 25, 2021, began with Shri Ram Madhav, Member, Board of Governors, India Foundation, introducing the speaker Shri Sajad Lone. Shri Lone is a politician from the Valley. He has been a minister in the past, and he heads a party called the Jammu and Kashmir People's Conference.

Sajad Lone began his speech by telling the audience about his political journey. Sajad's father had also been a senior politician. He had started as a member of the Congress Party, but died as a separatist. He had been killed by terrorists in

2002. In contrast, Sajad had started as a separatist, and had then gravitated towards the mainstream.

Sajad Lone then began to touch upon the issues afflicting Jammu and Kashmir today. He set the tone for the rest of his session by telling the audience that statehood had been snatched from his land. He told the audience that it was an outsider who was taking care of his state, and that this was not the case with the other states from which most members of the audience belonged, since those states had their own elected state governments.

Sajad Lone then spoke about how patriotic the common Kashmiri was. He narrated many anecdotes to demonstrate that despite the forces that were attempting to break the region away from India, it was the common Kashmiris who were ensuring that the region in fact remained a part of India. From fighting the Pakistani raiders in 1947 to the 25,000 Kashmiri Muslims who had sacrificed their lives as part of the security forces through the decades, he told the audience that these were the people who had ensured that Kashmir had remained an integral part of India. He told the audience that each one of them knew terrorist Burhan Wani's name but not that of any Kashmiri Muslim who was martyred fighting for India. He asked the audience to reflect on the role the media and fundamentalists had played.

Despite such exemplary patriotism, the Indian state had snatched statehood away from the region and made it a Union Territory. He told the audience that the people did not deserve this after working in India's interests for decades, and said that the Union Territory status made them feel ashamed. There were some "black sheep" who had colluded with Pakistan, he admitted. However, he cautioned the audience against painting all Kashmiri Muslims with a broad brush. He lamented the fact that despite their deeds being good, Kashmiri Muslims had little control over their words. This had constantly landed them in trouble, since people from the rest of India often considered them to be the enemy because of their rhetoric.

Sajad Lone then moved on to the abrogation of Article 370. He opined that this was a step that had had emanated from a strong ideological standpoint and there was not much that could be done about it. However, he returned to the issue of statehood, telling the audience that its withdrawal was neither ideological nor necessary. The Kashmiri Muslim, according to him, was caught between a rock and a hard place. If he took a bullet for India, he lost his life. If he did not, he was considered to be the enemy. He appealed to the audience not to judge the Kashmiri Muslims through one prism, and told the audience that it was important to unlearn some of the misconceptions they had lived with. He stressed on the importance of learning to unlearn, which according to him, was the most important form of learning.

Sajad Lone then made an emotional appeal to the audience. He said India was not a nation of Hindus and Muslims, but a nation of mothers and sisters, of brothers and fathers. He appealed for compassion across the board. Article 370 was not a symbol of superiority over the rest of India, he claimed. In fact, it symbolised that Jammu and Kashmir was actually India's special child. He repeated that from being the most special child or the most powerful state, India had relegated the region to Union Territory status. He then reiterated that he was not expecting India to restore Article 370, but the least India could do was to restore statehood. He told the audience that they needed to remind themselves that not everyone was out to undermine Indianness.

Sajad Lone's speech was followed by a question-and-answer session. Shri Ram Madhav began the proceedings by asking Sajad if he had any regrets about the fact that he had ditched the separatist bandwagon and joined mainstream forces. Sajad answered that he had none. It was part of his journey. He said that he did not always agree with what he saw in the mainstream bandwagon, but he had seen much worse when he was part of the separatist bandwagon, including bloodshed.

The floor was then opened to the audience. In the first round, he was asked about why the focus was not on constructive issues, why the Kashmiri Muslims had never come out and stood with the Kashmiri Pandits during their persecution, and what the regional parties had done to create awareness amongst the Kashmiri Muslim youth. He answered by first stating that he had never differentiated between Kashmiri Muslims and other Indians, that he viewed them all through the same prism. If someone did not, the onus to unlearn and relearn lay on them. He said it was an unfair charge on the Kashmiri Muslims as to why they had never stood with the Pandits during their persecution, because such questions were never asked to the Hindus of Delhi in the context of the 1984 Sikh pogrom. Once again, he brought up the issue of statehood, claiming that the scope for the region's development was huge, but a state government did not even exist to carry it out. Regarding the regional parties, Sajad said that the Congress Party had never allowed more than two parties to grow in the state, and that even the BJP had a soft corner for them. However, he admitted that the utterances of regional parties in Kashmir had to be moderate.

In the next round of questions from the audience, Sajad Lone was asked if he was happy about the outcome of the meeting that was held between the Kashmiri leaders and Prime Minister Modi, how he would incorporate 'Azadi' in his vision for the state, how could negative sentiments on the ground be changed, and whether he believed whether there were any advantages following the abrogation of Article 370. Sajad Lone answered that he was indeed happy about the meeting held with Prime Minister Modi. He said the leaders got a chance to place their points before the Prime Minister. He also added that the delimitation process that the Prime Minister spoke about was not an ideological process, but a bureaucratic or technical one. Responding to the question on 'Azadi', Sajad said that such things would have no place if Kashmir was in the safe hands of people such as himself and former Deputy Chief Minister Nirmal Singh, who was also part of the audience. Regarding the abrogation of Article 370, he said that he did not agree with the move as a Kashmiri, but categorically stated that the Union Government, elected democratically and with a brute majority no less, had been well within its rights to abrogate such a law.

The third round of questions began with a member of the audience questioning Sajad about his appeal to be compassionate because India was a country of mothers and daughters, on the basis of Kashmir's track record of double standards when it came to women. He was also asked about the Union Government's handling of the aftermath of Article 370's abrogation. Regarding Kashmir's track record of treating women poorly and how he was using 'mothers and daughters' to push his agenda now, Sajad said that if mistakes had been made in the past, we must consider them to be wrong. However, these mistakes must not be repeated. Regarding the abrogation of Article 370, Sajad reiterated that the Union Government had been well within its rights to abrogate it. He praised the government for preventing loss of life in its aftermath. However, he also stated that many other parts of the country faced a variety of crises and challenges, and asked why Article 370 had not been imposed elsewhere.

Shri Ram Madhav then asked Shri Sajad Lone about the government that he was in with the BJP and the PDP, which lasted for three years. He wanted to know what Sajad thought of the experiment. Sajad Lone began by saying he had a bad portfolio, leaving the audience in splits. Then Sajad Lone explained the pros and cons of the experiment. The BJP, being a part of the government in Jammu and Kashmir, was, according to him, an important milestone in India's history. Prior to this, nobody in the Valley would have ever teamed up with the BJP, but now, the BJP is no longer politically untouchable. He also said that he had asked for votes in Narendra Modi's name, and managed to come second in the Valley despite a pre-poll alliance with the BJP. According to Sajad Lone, the government worked well until Mufti Mohammad Sayeed was the Chief Minister. The state received a hefty financial package from the centre, and many new colleges and power projects were sanctioned. However, the subsequent administration negated many of the good works, and actively worked against him.

For the final question, Sajad Lone was asked what, according to him, had been the golden period of Kashmir. This was particularly relevant in the context of what Capt. Alok Bansal had stressed upon in his speech earlier, about how Kashmir had flourished in every walk of life between the ninth and the fifteenth centuries. Sajad however answered that Kashmir's golden period was yet to come.

Despite the audience largely disagreeing with Sajad Lone on most issues, the session became an important talking point amongst the audience. Clearly, Sajad had given them a lot of food for thought. The interaction with Sajad Lone, who will continue to play an important role in Kashmiri politics in the years to come, certainly broadened the perspectives on Kashmir held by young thinkers from across the country.

Plenary Session II: Jammu & Kashmir post 2014: Dr. Nirmal Singh

The session began with Dr. Singh making the audience understand why it is important to know Kashmir. History plays a vital role in understanding the present demand, issues and aspirations of Kashmir. He stated that Kashmiriyat finds its origins in Sufism and then moved on to modern regional politics of Kashmir. He asserted that the abrogation of Article 370 was not only physical, that is geographical integration of Kashmir with the rest of India, but also constitutional and legal integration with the conscience of people integrated with India. Article 35A discriminated against the women of Kashmir, as the land laws differentiated women of one part of the country with another. Not a single casualty on the day of the abrogation proves the law and order handling capabilities of the Government of India. He said that the priority of the people is changing from the security aspect to development. From hydropower to other infrastructure development projects that are already in progress, but because of the pandemic, will take some time. However, within two to three years ground level changes will be seen.

Panel Discussion I: Missing Narratives
- Shri Junaid Mattu, Mayor, Srinagar
- Ms. Sonam Mahajan, Activist
- Ms. Smriti Kak, Journalist
- Chair: Shri Ram Madhav, Member, Board of Governors, India Foundation

The panel discussion on "Missing Narratives" started with the introduction of the three speakers, namely, Shri Junaid Mattu (Mayor, Srinagar), Ms. Sonam Mahajan (Activist), and Ms. Smriti Kak (Journalist). This discussion consisted of different views on overlooked issues from the viewpoint of the current Mayor, a Dogra, and a Kashmiri Pandit, respectively. The session was chaired by Shri Ram Madhav.

Ms. Smriti Kak began her speech by explaining the missing narrative of Kashmiri Pandits. The threat of unhappiness and anger that binds all the Kashmiri Pandits is often neglected. The emotional threat of having lost their homes, the economic fear of being unemployed for a long time, and the anger of distorted stories. This threat that continues through their stories represents the missing narrative of Kashmiri Pandits.

When the problem began, there were overnight blasts in Kashmir. There was fear, and the image of Kashmir as a serene, pristine place had changed to one of a battle ground. There was the loss of life of civilians, security, and military forces, all of which involved high human cost. At that time, the minorities were overlooked. Armed conflict continued till January 1990 and what was seen as *"Haalat Kharaab Ho Gaye"* across the borders led to a mass migration of people overnight. When this happened, it became very difficult to keep the stories of the Kashmiri Pandits on the fringes. Suddenly, Kashmiri Pandits were in the centre space when the level of trust was undermined leading to harassment of Kashmir Pandits, a situation in which it was difficult to ignore the community. Partition was not far behind in history; they have grandparents who lived through it, and they have been born and brought up listening to their heart-rending experiences. This was a re-enactment of something similar; people fearing for their homes and lives, and little recognition in the media. However, the story of the Kashmiri Pandits was not told as it should have been. There was patchy attention. So, essentially, what became the missing narrative now became the misleading narrative. People started aligning the stories with their political ideologies that suited their own narrative more. People from outside informed Kashmiri Pandits about their stories forgetting that they had witnessed it. Thus, their voice became a part of the misleading narrative that resulted in collateral damage. Many people came up with a contesting type of narrative of a fear psychosis. Amidst the political fight, ideological battle, and fight with Pakistan, their story began to get buried.

On the positive side, the community tried very hard to rebuild itself when all this was happening. This community took just a decade to rebuild its life, an achievement that sets it as an example or perseverance. However, the competitive narrative exists even now, where social media constantly highlights Kashmiri Pundits as vulnerable—for instance, comparing poor men's problems with that of Kashmiri Pandits. To understand the Kashmir problem, one needs to keep an open mind and talk to people. There is a unified threat that exists in families. There is a continuity in their stories about the uncertainty of returning to their homes. Over the period, governments have portrayed themselves as the saviour of Kashmiri Pandits. Of course, there relief packages have been announced and 5,000-6,000 jobs offered, but is that enough? Has the international community been nudged enough to realise the situation of Kashmiri Pandits in terms of their rehabilitation? These aspects need to be addressed. Furthermore, Ms. Kak suggests that this community does not seek revenge, but it is justice that they seek. Some people openly said that they were involved with the killing of Kashmiri Pandits. What they seek here is punishment as closure.

Ms. Kak encourages one to interact with people; they need to hear that Kashmiri Pandits do not exist in silence. Even after fleeing from Kashmir, they were tracked down and forced out of their homes in Jammu and Delhi. This led to not just emotional and social imbalance but also economic costs. Moving ahead, we need to build bridges among all the communities living in J&K to rebuild our lives. To do that, we need to bring the communities together on the same platform.

Ms. Sonam Mahajan started her speech by defining the Dogra identity. Dogra is not a religious identity; it is an ethno-linguistic community. They can be Hindus, Muslims, Christians, or Sikhs. When people talk about Kashmir; they do not talk of Jammu because mostly Kashmir is in the news for negative reasons. People tend to incline towards pessimistic news, but that needs to be changed. One should visit Jammu to realise that the social fabric there is completely different. Ms. Mahajan was raised in Rajouri town alongside Muslims. Her view regarding Kashmiri Pandits differed as in Rajouri they did not celebrate any festivals, be it Diwali, Holi and others without Muslims. They have always been together. She emphasised that J&K is not just about conflict; there is much prosperity. Even in Kashmir, there are many places where people live in harmony.

Ms. Mahajan revealed the exciting fact that most of the area occupied by Pakistan, apart from Gilgit-Baltistan, is Jammu. Whenever we talk about occupied territories, we mainly talk about PoK, but we must bring the missing narrative of Jammu out. That is because Pakistan, in international fora, has been projecting the case of occupied Kashmir. Pakistan claims that it had not occupied that area. Those were Muslim territories and the public was not happy with India due to which local rebellions existed. Of course, some places like Poonch had local rebellions due to the economic sanctions placed by the Maharaja, which was later turned into communal rebellion. Towns under Pakistani occupation, especially Mirpur, had considerable Hindu and Sikh populations. By highlighting the Hindu and Sikh populations in Pakistan-occupied areas, we can weaken Pakistan's case. Pakistan claims those areas based on the Muslim majority, which can be undermined.

Nevertheless, when we talk about PoJK, we only talk about Kashmir, not at all about Jammu. When we talk about Pakistan-occupied territories, one must understand that we do not just talk about Gilgit but also Jammu. We should be highlighting the significance of Jammu along with Kashmir with regard to PoJK.

Sri Junaid Mattu
Junaid Mattu is the Mayor of Srinagar as well as leader of Kashmir's 'Apni Party' and was called upon during the 'Missing Narratives' panel discussion to provide us with an insight into the minds of the local Kashmiri. He began his speech by acknowledging that Kashmir is a classic example of conflicting narratives that have gone on to mould and shape the collective history and narrative of the Kashmiri people, cutting across religious divides and linguistic barriers. He believes that there have mainly been two narratives regarding Article 370. Specifying them, he said

that on one end is the deeply entrenched, mainstream narrative, which believes that the special status of J&K protected and empowered the people of the state; it is one that has found a deeper psychological home and imprint in the minds of the Kashmiri people. The counter narrative, supported by the Central Government, states that the abrogation of Article 370 will lead to the economic, political, and social empowerment of the people and that the Constitution of India will safeguard the rights of the Kashmiri people.

After stating the two opposite sides of the spectrum, Junaid Mattu addressed the question 'What does the local Kashmiri feel about the decisions taken by the Central Government, namely, the dissolution of Article 370 and 35A?'

Personally, Shri Junaid firmly believes the argument that 'the abrogation of the special status will lead to the empowerment and economic prosperity and progress of the Kashmiri people' is an argument that needs to be made. He goes on to explain that Jammu and Kashmir is rife with stark ideological stances, however rational, progressive and forward thinking. The average Kashmiri seeks everything that his counterpart in Mumbai may seek—better quality of life, education, etc. He also believes that it is too soon after the abrogation of Article 370 to assess if these things have been achieved and that time will be the best judge.

Speaking about the stereotyping of the young Kashmiri that has been done in the past, he explains that it is this stereotyping that has led to the alienation of Kashmir from India. The mainstream media has not helped bridge that divide, rather it has widened it. The shrillest, most unrealistic and, ironically, un-recruited voices find amplified spaces in the mainstream media and these are the voices which are hyperbolically on either side of the cultural divide. These hyperbolic positions have left a psychological imprint on the psyche of the young Kashmiri. Junaid Mattu goes on to then question the audience "This Young Thinkers Meet, a collection of eclectic minds from all over the country, is the idea of India. But how many Kashmiris have had exposure to such a Meet?" Here is where the challenge lay pre-August 2019, and here is where it still lies.

Junaid Mattu goes on to bring to light the importance of not oversimplifying narratives and cliches because it tends to offend Kashmiris in the process of oversimplifying their collective, inherited legacy—from what they've suffered over the years to the conflict and turmoil they've had to endure in the past decades. Every young Kashmiri wants a better future for himself and his children. To assume anything contrary would be based on illogical beliefs. But when we oversimplify his apprehensions, we also oversimplify his aspirations, running into a risky trajectory of further alienating that young Kashmiri. He firmly affirms that he believes in reform and asks us to not call this reform 'Naya Kashmir.' He reiterates how India is a magnanimous country, one that accommodates linguistic barriers and religious beliefs, dialectical differences and cultural differences, forming the very essence of the nation. To bring this perception of India to the young people of Jammu and Kashmir, we need to appreciate the uniqueness of the cultural, social and political legacy that the young Kashmiri has inherited. Thus, when we shelve this legacy into the realm of irrelevance and say that 'New Kashmir starts now and that the past will not affect what happens in the future', we tend to oversimplify that construct.

Junaid Mattu explains that the average Kashmiri, does, in fact, continue to be sceptical and cynical; however, he has sound reasons or unsound reasons, natural or synthesised, to believe so. Understanding what instigates his apprehension is how we will be able to save him from exploitation. The traditional mainstream has exploited the people of Kashmir over the decades, fighting elections on a fear psychosis. As a result, Kashmir has suffered from rampant miss-governance over the decades. Elections in Kashmir have rarely been fought on factors such as the Growth Development Index of the state; rather, they have been fought on the basis of instilling fear in the people.

He concluded his speech by saying that the future lies in accommodating the angst and anguish inside a young Kashmiri in the idea of India. As long as we all believe that the future of Jammu and Kashmir lies within the idea of India and accommodate the perceptive discrepancies in our idea of India, we can all find similarities in our thoughts. By telling the young Kashmiri 'we can agree to disagree', being accommodating and magnanimous, we will be able to usher Jammu and Kashmir across religious, linguistic and sectarian divides and move towards holistic development.

Plenary Session IV

- Ms. Sheena Nab Abs, SAP, Rajouri
- Shri Reyes Mohammad Bhat, SSP, Baramulla
- Chair: Shri Alok Bansal, Director, India Foundation

Sheema Qasba began by sharing how her upbringing and early years in Srinagar have shaped her perspective. She has seen the challenges faced by the Valley from a very young age:

* she had to deal with terrorism unlike any other cadre. Terrorism is often given a straightjacket view, but there is diversity and context in each case, it varies from place to place. With every passing year in service since 2018, she had seen its contours, dynamics and responses change. J&K is a vast area, the challenges vary among and within borders, and hinterlands.

* Mixed populations reside together which brings its flavour and challenges. Sensitivities are involved and evolving related to the issues of co-existence. People take pride in the dialects and diversity that have existed for years. The festivities provide an insight into the combined taste of celebrations.

* Need to innovate every day. New forms of technology are finding their way into terrorism, and they have to be a step ahead in dealing with the evolving trends.
* COVID posed unique challenges. People still wanted to continue their festivities, the police were in charge of facilitating safe ways of conducting rituals. They also led resource mobilisation like oxygen cylinders and helplines for COVID patients. The team saw humanity at its worst, but stepped up to support, which built trust within the community.
* Departments must take initiatives at any level they can. Building trust within the community through activities, big or small, has been essential. Small activities add up over time and have a snowballing impact.
* Dealing with drug abuse has been an increasing challenge. The police are running two de-addiction centres in JK with continuous outpatient treatment, leading to improved trust and social capital within the community.

A celebrated officer with many accolades for his bravery and commitment, Rayees Bhat also reflected on his childhood and candidly shared personal anecdotes to highlight the complex realities of J&K and the impact that they have had on him.

Kashmir is a small valley, where people know each other, and live in a shared fabric of culture. However, when he visited Jammu, it was very different from the fabric he had grown in; he was welcomed with a high culture shock. He was refused admission by the principal for being a Kashmiri, the college was reserved for those from Jammu. He did not give up and found himself a seat. This was a start of a journey towards an integrated J&K, without internal reservations and divides.

His friend's perception towards Kashmir was another trigger in his life. When the Mumbai attacks happened, there was a fear that Kashmir might be in danger too. No one was thinking about Kashmiris, people who are constantly living in fear, trying to manage perception, and carving a place to live.

Mr. Rayees underlined the importance of building bridges to combat distrust and overcoming individual challenges to focus on a collective. Kashmir needs a strong leadership that provides resources, exposure and builds trust.

Plenary Session V: Regional Politics with National Outlook: Shri Altaf Bukhari

Shri Altaf Bukhari prominently talked about regional parties and their connection with national politics. Jammu and

Kashmir being culturally diverse, the abrogation of Article 370 was a sudden shock for the people here. The J&K Apni Party came into existence when people of Jammu and Kashmir were at the crossroads. He was critical of the families that misruled this state for 72 years. There were many emotional issues across the borders. So, coming at a stage where people were hurt, there was a severe need for national integration. When Article 370 was incorporated in the Constitution of India, leaders at the helm of affairs should have made people aware that this was temporary. No progress was made for 72 years. It was the people of Jammu and Kashmir who said *"Khabardar hoshiyar hum Kashmiri hai taiyar"*.

Even two years after the abrogation of Article 370, there were no effective steps or integration of people here. Unless that happens, the desired results will not materialise. He emphasised the fact that we need to create an interest in the people of Jammu and Kashmir about the economics of India. Also, students and youngsters should not stop at Lakhanpur and it should not be their barrier to grow academically. Why should someone from Jammu and Kashmir be treated differently than those of other states as they have the same constitutional rights. He called upon the delegates at the YTM to be ambassadors of New J&K. Shri Bukhari urged everyone to maximise efforts in bringing the people of J&K into the mainstream.

He talked about the integration of hearts and minds and not only land. The Apni Party was born out of the fear in the minds of people, the fear of the lost identity which J&K people were having. The sentiment was not against India but how the abrogation will be implemented. Starting from 5 September, the Apni Party tried to calm the fear among people and with steadfast efforts from 23 December onwards they have started seeing changes amongst the public who were opposing the abrogation and now accepting it. On 3 January, they had conducted a survey that revealed that 7/10 were opposing and 3/10 were supporting. After 45 days, 4/10 were supporting them. In the meeting of 24 June, when the PM invited suggestions from all the local parties, there was a feeling of integration among the people here. On 7 July, it was 5/5 people supporting the abrogation. People gradually understood the fact of integration. For the regional parties, the core issues were the same; land protection, statehood, culture, jobs. Regional politics with a national outlook can bring about the best solutions for these issues. It was with this vision that Apni Party has put in all its efforts to work for the national interest. Every state, wherever there is a regional party, be it West Bengal, Maharashtra or Jammu and Kashmir, focus should be placed on local issues but not at the cost of neglecting the national interest. The main task of such parties is to see how they co-exist.

He ended on a very good note by saying the most important part is the national interest where we people can bring the people of Jammu and Kashmir into the mainstream, be it in employment, health care, education, tourism and all other sectors through national integration.

(Mock Parliament Session at the Young Thinkers Meet)

Interaction Session: Shri Arun Kumar Mehta, Chief Secretary, Jammu & Kashmir

Shri Arun Kumar Mehta, in his brief interaction, stated that the year 1990 marked the abject surrender of state authority in Jammu & Kashmir. The elections that followed were watershed in nature. From that time, the state and its apparatus has come a long way. He further stated that Article 370 acted against the very idea of India. After the Article was abrogated, transparency has improved due to a change in the administration's culture and, most importantly, the third tier of government in the state has been empowered.

INDEX

A
Abdullah, Sheikh, 43
Administrative Corruption, 45
Afghanistan, 13
Agriculture, 58
AK56, 74
Akbar, M.J., 74
All India Institutes of Medical Sciences (AIIMS), 51
Almonds, 57
al-Qaeda, 13
Amarnath, 26
Apples, 57, 59
Article 35A, 28, 30, 49, 51, 54, 69, 100
Article 370, 8, 16-18, 24, 28, 30, 34, 36, 38-39, 49, 51, 53-55, 67, 69, 79, 90, 96, 99
Atmanirbhar (self-reliant), 59
Atrocities against Kashmiris, 82
Azaadi, 33

B
Babasaheb Ambedkar, 48
Budget, Estimation, Allocation, Management System model, 24, 45
Bhagavata Gita, 96

BJP-PDP alliance, 18
Bukhari, Altaf, 19, 90
Burhan Wani, 73, 83

C
Capital Interest Subvention, 60
Capital Investment Incentive, 60
China, 7, 13
Confused, 23
Congress Party, 18
COVID-19, 5
Crisis Management, 64
CRPF, 31, 72, 73, 74, 80, 91
CVK Group, 59

D
Dal Lake, 24, 56, 91
Dalmia Cements, 59
Democracy, 40
Department for Promotion of Industry and Internal Trade (DPIIT), 59-60
Detached Approach, 46
Development, 39, 70
  Projects, 64
  with Dignity, 47
Development, Consensual and Inclusive Model, 47
Developmental Front, 43

Developmental Turn, 44
E
Economic Infrastructure, 64
Education, 70
Employment, 39
F
fauji, 89
G
Ghulam Ali Lone, 91
Gilgit Baltistan, 40
Gilgit Buddha, 39
Goods and Service Tax, 60
Government of India (GoI), 50-52
Great Indian Dream, 3
Gross State Domestic Product (GSDP), 57-58
GST Linked Incentive, 61
Gulmarg, 66
Gupkar Alliance, 20, 53, 55
H
Handicrafts, 58
Haqqani network, 13
haraamis, 76
haram, 76
Himalayas, 88
Hukus Bukus, 85
Human Development Index, 65
Humanitarian Relief, 64
I
Impacting the National Discourse, 3
Improving Infrastructure, 70
India, 7, 24, 28, 40, 43, 57, 68
India-2047, 3
Indian Army, 73
Indian Democracy@2030, 3
Infant Mortality Rate (IMR), 50

Islamic State (IS), 13
Islamists' *jihad*, 68
IT Sector, 40
IT Servers, 40
J
Jaish-e-Mohammed, 13
Jakson Group, 59
Jamhuriyat, Insaniyat with Kashmiriyat, 46
Jammu, 36
Jammu & Kashmir (J&K), 7-9, 11-12, 14, 27, 29, 35, 38, 43, 46, 49, 51
Counter Terrorism force, 88
Jammu & Kashmir Infrastructure Development Finance Corporation (JKIDFC), 64
Jammu and Kashmir AYUSH Care Investment Policy-2020, 63
Jammu and Kashmir Captive Power Policy-2020, 62
Jammu and Kashmir Government, 59
Jammu and Kashmir Hydro Power and Renewable Energy Policy-2020, 63
Jammu and Kashmir Police (JKP), 31-32, 76, 89
Jammu and Kashmir Tourism Policy-2020, 62
Jannat, 55, 75
jihad, 31
JK Public Works, 45
K
Kashmir, 16, 21-24, 26-27, 33-34, 47, 67-68, 71, 76, 80

Separatist Movement, 93
Willow, 80
Kashmiri Fare, 90
Kashmiri *kehwa*, 73
Kashmiri Pandit Sangharsh Samiti (KPSS), 54
Kashmiri Pandits, 36, 54, 68, 93
Kashmiri Subalterns, 45
Kashmiriyat, 38-39, 46
Khelo India Winter Games, 66
Know Kashmir, 3, 67

L

Ladakh, 36
Ladakh Standoff, 13
Lal Chowk, 17
Lashkar-e-Mustafa, 13
Lashkar-e-Taiba, 13
Lata Mangeshkar, 94

M

Maharaja Hari Singh, 82
Martyr, 56
Maternal and Child Healthcare, 50
Maternal Mortality Ratio (MMR), 50
Mattu, Abdul, 72
Medical Care, 70
Mijaaz nahin milta mera, 78
mijaaz, 78
Militancy, 17
Modi, Narendra, Prime Minister, 18, 66
Moksopaya Shastra, 82

N

namaz, 76
National Family Health Survey (NFHS), 50
National Highway Infrastructure Development Corporation (NHIDCL), 65
National Interest, 5
Nationalism vs. Separatism, 23
Nationalistic, 23
Naxal (anti-establishment), 87
Naya Kashmir, 49, 51-52, 113
Nehru, Pandit, 68
Neonatal Intensive Care Units (NICUs), 51
Neonatal Mortality Rate (NMR), 50
New Age Leadership, 3
New India: Ideas, Concepts and Contestations, 3

O

OMMAS (Online, Management, Monitoring and Accounting System), 45
Overground Workers (OGWs), 10

P

Pahalgam, 19
Pakistan, 7, 42, 69, 75
Pakistan-occupied Kashmir (PoK), 36, 68, 100
Pakistan-sponsored Insurgency, 68
Panchayat Raj system, 70
Paperboat and Design Studios Private Limited, 59
Paradigm Shift, 45
Patel, Sardar, 43
Patriotism Test, 47
Pir Panjal, 78, 88
Pradhan Mantri Surakshit Matritva Abhiyan (PMSMA), 51

Index

Prime Minister's Development Package (PMDP), 63, 91
Progressive Solutions, 47
purnahuti, 96

R

Radical Elements, 46
Radicalisation, 23, 68
Renaissance Painting, 92
Road-Operating-Party, 80

S

Saffron, 57
Sajad Lone, 19, 100, 102
Samudra Manthan (Churning of the Ocean), 96
Security Tracker Project, 9
Sentimental and Emotional Issues, 47
Shankaracharya, 81
Shardapeeth, 39, 81
Shastra Seema Bal (SSB), 87, 89
Shiva temple, 92, 96
Shree Cements, 59
shruti, 82
Sick Newborn Care Units (SNCUs), 51
Skilled Birth Attendance (SBA), 51
smriti, 82
Social Infrastructure, 64
Soft Corner, 43
Splendid Paradise, 42
Srinagar, 90
Switzerland of the East, 57

T

Taliban-Afghanistan Conundrum, 13
talkhi (bitterness), 92
Tantraloka, 81
terrorist, 56
Total Fertility Rate (TFR), 50
Tso Moriri Lake, 94

U

Udhampur, 89
UN Security Council, 68
Under-five Mortality Rate (U5MR), 50
UNESCO, 71
Union Government/Central Government of India, 8, 28-30, 34, 41, 70, 104-5, 112
Union Ministry of Health and Family Welfare, 49
Union Territory (UT), 23, 29, 31, 36, 49, 56, 62, 65, 70, 99-102
United Nations Military Observation Group, 53

V

Vaishno Devi, 26
Vajpayee, Atal Bihari Ji, late Prime Minister, 46

W

Walnuts, 57
Working Capital Interest Incentive, 61

Y

yagna, 96
Young Thinkers Meet (YTM), 2-3, 5, 21, 23, 35, 38-39, 44, 67, 118

Z

Zabarwan Range, 92
Zojila Tunnel, 65